Eating Nebraska

A Humorous Guide to Dining in the Cornhusker State

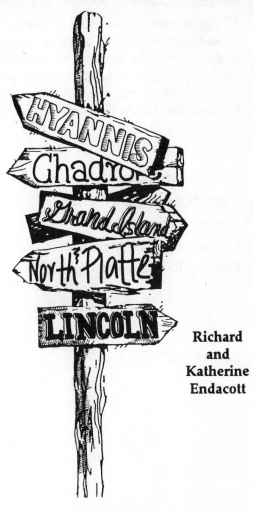

Richard
and
Katherine
Endacott

Pleasant Dale Press
Route One, Box 120A
Pleasant Dale, Nebraska 68423

Cover Design: Les Remmers
Illustrations: Monica Mercer
Layout: Angie Johnson
Production: Linda Messman
Printing: Record Press, Cairo, NE

ISBN 0-9627861-0-1

CONTENTS

CONTENTS

CONTENTS

CONTENTS

CONTENTS

Introduction

From a modest beginning—a dinner date at the El Toro Lounge in Crete—a pastime has evolved into a passion for sharing experiences that are quintessential Nebraska—auctions, county fairs, church suppers, small-town parades, corn-picking contests, flea markets, 10K road races, antique shops, eight-man football, big city ethnic festivals, and family-run restaurants.

In our travels about the state, we've delighted in discovering unique eateries. With no culinary road map to guide us, we've used a hit-or-miss approach to dining. (A tactic that can result in memorable meals, and some we wish we could forget!) Our meals have sometimes been burned in the freezer and then tanned in the microwave. Yet for every salad of warm, brown lettuce and every heavy-weight stack of pancakes there are scrumptious suppers prepared and served with care. But you need to be a supper scout to know where to look.

Our research began with a questionnaire for business leaders asking their advice about the best and most unique eating places. We also searched through countless newspaper articles and made inquiries of people around the state. All the while we continued to sample restaurants (more than 350), put miles on the ole buggy (20,000), and in the words of our doctor, eat ourselves into an early grave.

Some fifteen pounds later, we selected the 130 spots included in *Eating Nebraska*. Mind you, these are not necessarily the best places in the state (How can you compare a cafe in Gurley with a continental bistro in Omaha?), but you'll find all the places in this book are one-of-a-kind in terms of atmosphere, food, history, or service (or lack of any of the above).

The reviews and essays are a little irreverent, but most food and restaurant writers take their work too seriously these days. Just toss this book in the glove compartment of your car and follow us. We'll have you singing around a campfire near Chimney Rock and eating in what was formerly a bookie's joint in South Omaha. You'll taste corn nuggets in Eustis, verenika in Henderson, and empanadas in Omaha. We'll introduce you to the Greek who is king of the Coney Island hot dog and a talented Lithuanian who specializes in Jewish home cooking. We'll even show you where to get a good five cent cup of coffee and direct the hungriest of you to Harrison, home of the twenty-eight-ounce hamburger.

In our reviews, we've purposely omitted hours of operation (they change almost daily). Please call ahead. It can be downright maddening to arrive with the tummy on empty only to find the cafe closed.

Since restaurant picking is a matter of taste, we realize you're not always going to agree with our favorites. You may feel that your son-in-law's place is better than our choice, and you may even find that eating at one of our picks is as pleasant as going on a ten-mile hike ... with a blister. But be tolerant; all cooks can have an off day. Anyway, part of the fun of cross-country food ferreting is not knowing for sure what you'll find. In fact, we want to know what you think. With all the extra pounds we've put on during this project, we've become pretty thick skinned. So send your supper scout tips to the Endacotts: Route 1, Box 120A, Pleasant Dale, Nebraska 68423.

NORTHWEST REGION

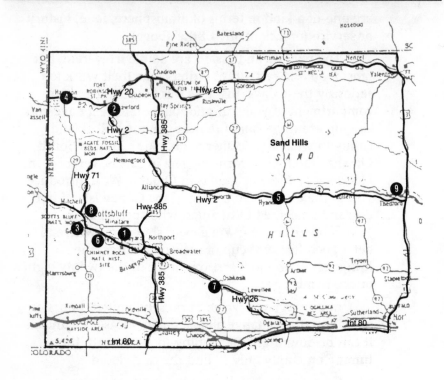

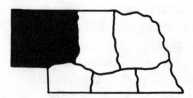

Northwest

1. Bayard—Oregon Trail Wagon Train
2. Crawford—O'Doherty's
3. Gering—Bush's Gaslight
4. Harrison—Sioux Sundries
5. Hyannis—Hyannis Hotel Bar
6. Melbeta—The Flame
7. Oshkosh—The Market
8. Scottsbluff—El Charrito
   (also Pepe's, Rosita's)
9. Thedford—The Cowpoke Inn

The Cafe Litmus Test

An Essay

You drive into a strange town. You're tired and hungry for some good food, but how do you find THE best place to eat? Calvin Trillin, author of *American Fried: Adventures of a Happy Eater,* describes the problem this way: "Despite the best efforts of forward-looking bankers and mad-dog franchisers, there is still great food all over the country, but the struggle to wring information from the locals about where it is served can sometimes leave a traveler too exhausted to eat."

Trillin recommends the food interrogation technique when searching for the best cafes. I usually try this at my first stop—the local filling station. In response to

subtle questions, the fellow pumping gas usually says something like, "Go to Ernie's. Best damn place around. Drive down this street to the ole Johnson place—it's a big green house with a porch. Turn left and go one more block to Ernie's. Ya can't miss it." Translation: "Ernie's is the *only* place around, and I have the same love for grease that French cooks have for sauce."

After trying this method on several occasions, I developed a suspicion about gas station attendants as unbiased advisors. This suspicion was heightened when, after one particularly bad meal at a recommended spot, I discovered that my informant's girlfriend worked at the joint he had so enthusiastically recommended. Conflicts of interest taint even the food field.

A friend of mine who owns a restaurant in Lincoln says he drives into a strange town and locates the cafe with the most pickups parked out front. I've tried it. It doesn't work. This test will only prove that the place has the cheapest coffee in town, not necessarily the best hot beef sandwich. It can also mean that the owner has the help, their families, and all of his friends park their vehicles in front. I once stopped at a place that had four pickups and two cars parked in front of it. Yet when I walked inside, it was as crowded as most offices are at 5:05 p.m.

> A friend of mine drives into a strange town and locates the cafe with the most pickups parked out front.

Another touted technique is the faded sign test. This test is based on the notion that if the sign out front is faded, the place has been in business for a long time. I tried this test recently. The faded oval-shaped sign proclaimed: "GAS" horizontally and "EAT" vertically, cleverly arranged so that a single "A" was used in both. (I learned, much too late, that the sign held a hidden meaning.) After sitting down, the first thing I noticed was the directions for the Heimlich maneuver printed on the front of the menu. The meal itself was also unsettling. When I couldn't finish the chicken-fried steak, I asked for a doggie bag; they brought me an airsick bag. Paying my bill, I noticed that rather than mints next to the cash register, there was a bowl of Bloat-Guard. So much for the faded sign test.

One of the more intriguing tests is advanced by author William Least Heat Moon. In his best seller, *Blue Highways*, Least Heat Moon writes that the most infallible way of picking a cafe is to peer in the window and count wall calendars:

No calendar: Same as an interstate pit stop.

One calendar: pre-processed food assembled in New Jersey.

Two calendars: only if fish trophies are present.

Three calendars: can't miss on the farm boy breakfasts.

Four calendars: try the ho-made pie, too.

Five calendars: keep it under you hat or they'll franchise it.

I tried this theory on a central Nebraska cafe having no less than 166 current calendars on the wall. There were calendars from Coca-Cola to the Caselli Insurance Co. and from the Bank of Odell to the Bank of America. Based on the Least Heat Moon test, I was peering into a five-star restaurant.

> . . .the most infallible way of picking a cafe is to peer in the window and count wall calendars.

But no-ooo. There was some kind of critical mass at work here. First of all, the Calendar Cafe reminded me of my Aunt Salli's kitchen. (Our family claimed her house was so messy that burglars could ransack it and she'd never notice.) At the very least, the owner should have placed a ladder in the middle of the dining room with a sign saying, "Pardon our mess, we're redecorating." My better judgement suspended by extreme hunger, I sat down next to a calendar with a white bull advertising Devon Dells Charolais Ranch at Pleasant Dale. The table was decrepit, set with stained utensils, a crinkled paper napkin, and an orange plastic water glass that looked like it had spent the better part of a week tumbling in a cement mixer.

The waitress finally quit fussing with her beehive hairdo to come over to take my order. Staring straight ahead, comatose-like, she mumbled, "What kin I git ya, honey?" I ordered something simple—a large orange juice, french toast, and coffee. The waitress shuffled back across the room and bellowed in a bullhorn voice, "The dude wants O.J. in the air, a frenchie, and a bucket of mud." She sneezed while placing the order in front of me, then wiped her nose on the frilly hanky in her blouse pocket, and cooed, "Here ya go, hon, just what ya wanted." Those aren't the words I'd have chosen. The French toast was the consistency of Wonder Bread, a brand that I discovered early in life just does not stand up well to liquid. The cook had slapped the soggy bread on the griddle and produced a black char on the outside. Char can be tasty on Cajun red fish, but not on French toast, particularly when the char is combined with a mushy center. I tried to wash it down with coffee that had the color and taste of an oil slick. The only thing warm about the meal was the water.

This was a truly unforgettable meal—I could taste it with every belch for the next ten days. It succeeded in putting an eager eater like me completely off my feed (at least for a few minutes). Based on that adventure, I also decided that home cooking isn't necessarily good. In fact, if my mom had cooked like that, I'd have left home sooner.

Such disappointing and distasteful experiences have convinced me that most eatery tests, including Least Heat Moon's, don't quite fill the bill. So the Endacott theory of effective food ferreting goes something like this:

When you walk into a strange Nebraska eatery, look for the Cornhusker football schedule. (Don't

worry. There's always one somewhere.) The closer it is
to the cash register, the better the food. If the schedule's
on the back of the cash register, the hamburgers are top
notch. If the schedule has the up-to-date scores penciled in (as if anyone in the state had to look at a
schedule to learn the score of the games), you've discovered an eatery that'll compete with any in the
country. Try this test. So far it has worked every time.

Oregon Trail Wagon Train—Bayard

308-586-1850

In 1848, Father DeSmet, an early Nebraska ex-
plorer, described Chimney Rock, near present-
day Bayard: "One of the most remarkable curiosities of
this savage region...it is 175 yards above the plain and
may be perceived from thirty miles away." Gordon
Howard and his family operate one of Nebraska's most
unusual outdoor restaurants in the shadow of this sign
post on the Oregon Trail.

Gordon is the grandson of a fur trader, and his
family has lived on land adjacent to Chimney Rock for
over one hundred years. Thickly whiskered, tanned,
and sturdily built, he has the look of frontiersmen Jim
Bridger or Kit Carson, the visible strength and en-
durance of the wagon train drivers of long ago, and the
gregarious personality of an entertainer. There's some
professor in him too; he reveres the history of this area
and enjoys sharing his extensive knowledge with his
guests.

In addition to western outdoor cookouts in the summer, the Howard's operation also provides living-history wagon treks by reservation. These can last from three hours to six days. "We want people to understand how it really was, not how it is in the movies. It's pretty authentic, except for the chemical toilets. No use being miserable." Gordon says with a grin.

Chimney
Rock
Bayard

If you go for the chuck wagon steak dinner, held everyday except Thursday during the summer, plan to arrive early so you can ride in a mule-drawn conestoga wagon for a close-up view of Chimney Rock. After the wagon ride, there is time for a beverage and a leisurely stroll along the Platte River or through the Howards' scenic grounds, once a favorite camping spot for wagon trains.

As chow time neared, the night Katherine and I visited the Howard's establishment, a hungry group of observers gathered around the open grill. We were entertained by Gordon's impromptu banter while he and a crew of helpers adroitly broiled seventy thick, juicy ribeye steaks.

The meal which greeted our appetites, whetted in the open air, was exceptional: steaks, baked potatoes, relishes, creamed green beans, sourdough bread, and homemade ice cream. We ate at rough picnic tables set under a timber shelter. The food was so plentiful and satisfying that I want to go back one Thursday when the Howard's serve an authentic pioneer cookout menu: trail stew, hoecakes, spoonbread, relishes, sourdough bread, and vinegar pudding. In the winter the operation moves to a nearby cabin and serves prime rib by the light of lanterns and a huge fireplace.

A campfire with an old-fashioned sing-a-long led by Gordon and a grizzled, guitar-playing sidekick ended the pleasant evening. Gordon's face glowed like a fiddler's at a hoedown as he joked and led the songs. His contagious enthusiasm and wholesome humor quickly turned a group of strangers into old friends.

It was dark when the campfire-sing ended. The group strolled back to the parking lot commiserating about how it hurt to laugh on a full stomach. An illuminated Chimney Rock stood before us, not as tall now as Father DeSmet described it, but still an impressive reminder of Nebraska's rich western heritage.

308-665-1725

"T he finest cuisine and atmosphere between Lincoln and Denver." That's what some say about O'Doherty's in Crawford. And the plaudits continue: "For culinary and wine delight include O'Doherty's at Crawford...whose breadth of menu and price values best Omaha's Old Market." (Joe Seacrest, president of Lincoln Journal-Star Printing Co.). One English travel writer went so far as to exclaim: "Super. Worth traveling 6,000 miles!"

Fortunately, Nebraskans don't have to travel quite that far to get to O'Doherty's, but whatever the distance, it's worth the trip. O'Doherty's has it all: old West atmosphere, history, great variety in its food, and friendly northwest Nebraska service.

Let's start with the area. Crawford is located in the heart of Nebraska's frontier. It was at Fort Robinson, just outside of Crawford, that Crazy Horse, perhaps the most celebrated figure in American Western history, was murdered. The fort was also the home of the Ninth and Tenth Cavalries, composed entirely of black soldiers. Cheyenne bands were imprisoned there, then escaped in a fatal attempt at freedom; the sad story of Wounded Knee took place only seventy miles north of Crawford. After the Indian Wars, the fort housed the K9 Corps, served as the practice area for the U.S. Olympic Equestrian Team, and as a prison for German soldiers captured during World War II.

The building which houses O'Doherty's was built in 1909 as the largest general store west of Lincoln. The original walls and the pressed-tin ceilings remain. The wide fir floorboards, patched with white pine and oak, were carefully refinished to save the holes through which rope was drawn up from the basement during its general store days.

The wonderful, ornate bar was brought from South Dakota, where it had been shipped by rail and ox teams in 1889. A penciled notation on the inside of one of its compartments reads: "pints, 3 cents—quarts, 4 cents."

The huge main dining room with its high ceilings recalls an antique mess hall. The walls are covered with western memorabilia—photos of cowboys, native Americans, pioneer families, saddles, and farming and cooking implements. There are handmade quilts hung on the walls alongside Indian artifacts.

The sliding doors to the dining room are from the old Chadron Opera House, and the front of the bar is faced by the fronts of opera boxes.

Diners are seated on a variety of locally collected chairs from the period 1880 to 1920. The area is made comfortable by red carpeting and blue tablecloths.

But there's more than just old West atmosphere at O'Doherty's. There's great food. The menu emphasizes the great beef produced in the ranching area that surrounds Crawford. Choices include chateaubriand, crab, trout, chicken Kiev, and lamb. In the summer on Fridays and Saturdays they serve a smorgasbord.

When I was last in Crawford, I tried just a little bit of several items on the menu, including some excellent beef, an unusual but delicious Indian taco, fresh-baked breads, and a relish tray with local summer vegetables. They also offer nine different kinds of potatoes. In the interest of valid testing, I sampled four of them at one meal: calico with peppers and tomatoes; sunrise, which were like hash browns with cheese; an unusual type of fried potatoes; and cross-cuts. (All that's left to test are

French fries, baked, curly fries, wedges, and American fries.)

In 1981 O'Doherty's received the Governor's Travel Award—the first time that the award had been given to a restaurant. Obviously, in my visit I found that the same high standards still exist. I agree with Jim Denny of the *Omaha World-Herald* who proclaims: "A trip to Fort Robinson and Crawford would not be complete without an evening at O'Doherty's."

Chewy Wilson

An Essay

"C rawford is famous for many things—Fort Robinson, O'Doherty's Restaurant, and Chewy Wilson. You've no doubt heard of the fort and the restaurant, but Chewy? Who in the heck's Chewy Wilson? Chewy is one of those characters who springs up out of the prairie and carries on as if he'd already experienced several lifetimes. In his life, Chewy was many things: businessman, author, philosopher, worm salesman, spitter, whittler, humorist—an unfortunate omission from *The Reader's Digest* list of most unforgettable characters.

> He was an unfortunate omission from *The Reader's Digest* list of most unforgettable characters.

I met Chewy several years ago as I was rummaging around Crawford looking for a good place to eat. At first glance I thought his place was a restaurant. When I looked closely, however, it was clear that it wasn't. The crudely painted letters on the front window read "Chewy Wilson's—Used Books and Wild Wurms." I went in anyway.

The place was dark, barely lit by daylight through the dirty front windows and a bare bulb hanging from a wire. No customers in sight, at least none that I could see. In the back of the store I noticed a grizzled old man with an unruly froth of white beard and hair, sitting in a rocking chair and whittling, his face a cross between Einstein and Rocky Graziano. Piles of junk and paperbacks, mostly Louis L'Amour westerns, surrounded him. As I approached, he looked up, but continued to whittle in silence. Then he turned his head to the side and lobbed a huge spitball of tobacco at the rusty spittoon near my right foot. Most of it missed the spittoon and, fortunately, also missed my foot. The token amount that did hit its mark was so diffused that it failed to register the "twiiinggg" that announces accuracy in this lost art. I noticed that quite a few had missed over the years. Backfire dribbles traced the front of his plaid shirt and purple tie. The plastered tobacco was a bit untidy, but it eased the transition from plaid to purple.

> The crudely painted letters on the front window read "Chewy Wilson's—Used Books and Wild Wurms."

"You Mr. Wilson?" I inquired.

The man responded with all the enthusiasm of a sleeping coon dog on an August afternoon. "Name's Wilson. Chewy Wilson." His voice was gravely—like a truck in low gear—and there was a surly twist to his upper lip. He punctuated his introduction with another lob in the direction of the spittoon. It landed low and to the left.

"Got any wild worms today?" I asked.

"Sheeoot, boy. What ya wantin' worms fer?"

"Thought I might do some fishing. By the way, how do you know they're wild?"

"Sheeoot, I been breedin' wild worms long before a squirt like you ever heared about a fishin' pole. I keep 'em wild by playin' loud rock music fer 'em at night. Plus I keep 'em active by puttin' shredded westerns in their box fer litter."

I walked around the room. The old barn-like building was filled with dusty books. Along one wall was a large wooden box marked "BEWARE. Open with care. Wild Wurms." I opened the lid, then closed it quickly. If I lived in a box that smelled like that, I'd be wild too.

I pulled up a wobbly three-legged stool a safe distance from the spittoon, and spent the next hour visiting with Chewy. During the course of our conversation, Chewy brought up the subject of teeth. He told me that he had the best-made set of false teeth in western Nebraska. That was another point I decided not to argue with him. But he insisted. "I've had them teeth fer twenty-five years, and I ain't even had to have 'em relined or overhauled or nothin'. Got 'em in the service. After the doc finished makin' my teeth I remembered the rule Sarge give us the first day we reported. He said to stencil all of your personal belongings for identification. So I had the Doc stencil my name on my uppers."

With that, he spat out the whole wad of tobacco into one hand and with the other he extracted his teeth. "Looky here, boy. See my name stenciled in the upper plate?" Sure enough, along the gum line—C. Wilson.

"Sure come in mighty handy too when I'm out of town. I use 'em for identification when I want to cash a check." Finally, he jammed the tobacco-stained teeth back into his mouth, along with the tobacco wad. "Ran into some trouble with 'em though one night in a bar over in Rushville."

"What sort of trouble?" I asked.

"Well, they had a smarty barmaid over there, big fat lady about fifty. She looked at my chompers, but refused to cash my check."

"Why?" I asked.

Chewy paused, his face growing even more serious than before, then continued, "Sheeoot, she said my teeth was nothin' but false identification."

With that Chewy smiled for the first time. In fact, he laughed so loud and long that he had a coughing fit. Tobacco spewed in every direction and he almost bucked out of his rocker. Then he suddenly quit coughing and laughing, his face turned solemn and he returned to his whittling. "Where's a good place to eat in Crawford?" I asked.

"Sheeoot," he said. "Ain't no place around this here area as good as O'Doherty's. It's as old as I am, and almost as good." Again he spat, and this time the spittoon registered a ringing hit. "Do you want me to take you over there?" he asked, as dribbles of his effort settled on his shirt and tie.

"No thanks," I said. "I think I'll wait awhile. I'm not very hungry right now."

Bush's Gaslight —Gering

308-632-7315

The Gaslight is a typical steakhouse, but it does have a very substantial menu or rather, a very substantial item on the menu—a twenty-ounce steak, proclaimed as one of Nebraska's best and biggest. As big as a catcher's mitt and tender as a marshmallow, it's appropriately dubbed "The Chunk."

I was eating there when a group of Japanese visitors stopped in while touring the state. I visited briefly with the man who was serving as tour guide. He whispered, "Watch this if you want to see some surprised looks." I sat at the next table and chatted with the visitors as they placed orders ranging from hamburger steak to filet mignon. Their host insisted that they sample some prize Nebraska beef.

When the orders arrived, in chorus, the visitors laughed and shouted their surprise. The waitress had placed a sizzling "Chunk" in front of each of the them.

When laughter subsided, the guide admitted that he had told the waitress to bring his guests the "Chunk," regardless of what they ordered. Most of them left with doggie bags. I've often wondered if any of the "Chunks" made it all the way back to Japan.

Sioux Sundries—Harrison

308-668-2577

Once upon a time, in the faraway village of Harrison, there was a food palace named Sioux Sundries. In this palace there lived a good and wise monarch of cooking, Queen Wasserburger. Outside of Harrison, in the wider kingdom of Sioux County, there lived a gentle giant, Rancher Coffee. Many stout-hearted men were employed by Rancher Coffee, but every day the men got very hungry and became very tired. The kind rancher tried everything he could to fill his hungry men, but try as he might, he couldn't satisfy them.

One day the enchanted jackelope of the Pine Ridge whispered into Rancher Coffee's ear, "Take your hard-working men to the palace of Queen Wasserburger." Rancher Coffee took his advice, and when he got there, he decreed," Puny hamburgers will not do. Fix my hungry men the biggest and best burgers in the land."

So Queen Wasserburger did. Each burger weighed twenty-eight ounces, measured six inches across, and spilled out all around the regular-size buns. She topped them off with onion, pickle, lettuce, cheese, mustard, and catsup...and a bag of cholesterol-free potato chips.

Rancher Coffee and his men ate and ate and ate, but they were unable to finish the huge burgers. They thanked the queen and walked out filled with renewed energy. From that time forward Rancher Coffee brought his men back to the palace every day to enjoy the giant burgers. News spread across the land, and the palace became famous for its giant "Coffee Burger." Rancher Coffee, the hard-working men, and Queen Wasserburger lived happily ever after.

※ ※ ※ ※

Today the guest book at Sioux Sundries includes signatures from all fifty states and fourteen foreign countries. For an eatery in a town of 360 located far from major population centers, that's quite an accomplishment. Plaques on the wall include the state tourism award and the Beef Backer Award from the Nebraska Beef Board. Sioux Sundries has been mentioned in *USA Today*, *Stars and Stripes*, and other publications and featured on Charles Kuralt's "Sunday Morning" (CBS).

Located on a corner of the main street, Sioux Sundries doesn't look like a restaurant. It isn't. It's a store where you can buy toothpaste, shampoo, bag balm, duct tape, kitchen knives, toys, graduation presents, diapers, photo albums, key rings, magazines, rain bonnets, videos, romance novels (new and used), and short-order meals. It's an antique Stop-and-Shop. If they don't have it, you don't need it.

The food can be found at the back in a tiny space large enough for five booths and a chrome-and-formica soda fountain counter. At 2:30 p.m. Katherine and I were the only customers, but by 3:00 p.m. twenty-five customers crammed into the booths for coffee and rolls or pie.

The Coffee burger was excellent—well-seasoned, flavorful, and not greasy. We asked the waitress the secret of the burgers. She claimed it was the freshness of the meat and admitted the size may add some novelty. "There may be a bigger burger somewhere," she said, " but until we find it, we're going to bill it as the world's largest." In our culinary travels, I've found nothing to dispute her claim.

The Hyannis Hotel Bar—Hyannis

308-458-2332

Big Red football dominates the conversation at most Nebraska bars. But at the famous Hyannis Hotel you won't hear much talk about red dogs, blitzes, or pulling guards. When they're talkin' sports at the hotel bar, they're most likely talkin ropin' calves, doggin' steers, and ridin' bulls or broncs. There are no Michael Jordan posters, no Royals baseball schedules, no Blackshirt pictures; the walls are covered with action photos of rodeo heroes—current ones like Skeeter Thurston, and J.W. Simondson and old-timers like Larry Mahan, Freckles Brown, and Shoat Webster. No Nikes or street shoes in there either, just sharp-toed boots, sometimes adorned with jangling spurs. Even the men's restroom is designated, "BULLS." Hyannis is hard-core cowboy country, and the Hyannis Hotel Bar is Nebraska's most authentic cowboy bar.

The bar is dark, dated, and worn, and its pace is laid back. In cow country it's not 9 to 5, it's until the work's done. The sign over the bar reflects this hard-working but easy-going attitude: "Bar Hours: Open most days about 8 or 10, occasionally as early as 7, but some days as late as 12 or 1." Another sign nearby says, "Cafe and Hotel open 24 hours." It's confusing, but I didn't have the guts to ask which one was correct. In cowboy country, dudes don't ask questions.

Hyannis
Hotel Bar
Hyannis

Not only is the bar interesting, the hotel itself is a landmark listed in the National Register of Historic Places. Built by Mrs. Rena Fair in 1898 in the French Empire style, it catered to local ranchers who brought their herds to Hyannis to load on the railroad.

I've never done any eating at the bar, but it's a fun place to have a cup of coffee or something stronger, sop up the atmosphere of the range, and rub elbows with Sandhills cowpokes.

The Hyannis Hotel is worth a visit. But remember, don't plan on asking about Big Red. If you do, you'll likely be offered a pouch of Red Man tobacco. In other words, when you walk into the bar, check your guns and watch your language. This is cowboy country.

The Flame—Melbeta

308-783-1727

I n 1971, the tiny town of Melbeta set a new record for per-capita contributions to the American Heart Fund drive—$4.08 per person. To celebrate, the townsfolks had an enormous feed at the local steakhouse. The cholesterol and calories consumed that night at the Flame must have soothed the consciences of those who felt that Melbeta had done too much to fight heart disease. The population of 151 consumed sixty pounds of lamb, thirty pounds of pork tenderloin, one hundred pounds of ham, twenty cans of lobster, and thirty cans of smoked octopus. Certainly more than your average steakhouse fare in both quantity and variety.

The Flame is a typical Nebraska steakhouse, but with a few extras on the menu. In addition to steaks, which run as large as twenty-two ounces, the Flame offers abalone, lobster, oysters, shrimp, smoked octopus, quail, escargot, trout, and frog legs. Sure, there are a lot of calories and cholesterol in all these goodies, but don't worry about that for once. When you get home you can ease your conscience with a large contribution to your local heart association.

308-772-4468

You've probably read about it in the newspapers. They say we should turn the Great Plains west of the ninety-eighth meridian into a huge national park and replace most of the people with buffaloes. They'd call it something catchy like "Buffalo Commons." That's the suggestion of two East Coast social scientists, Frank and Deborah Popper. These Great Plains experts live in New Jersey (nothing like being close to your subject). Their field of expertise is urban studies (an interesting background for dealing with rural problems). I suspect that when they decided to study the "Great Plains," they thought it involved observing the "great planes" at the Newark Airport.

Their Popper-cock theory proclaims that "Buffalo Commons" is the only feasible solution to Plains' problems of drought, cyclical markets, and depopulation. Great Plains folk reply, "What else is new?" These hardy people have wrestled with these problems for decades. And they've done much more than survive. They produce ninety percent of the country's grain-fed cattle, eighty-five percent of the grain sorghum, and fifty percent of the wheat, all from the same area that the Poppers propose to abandon. Great Plains residents can get mighty hot when Eastern dudes tell them they should move out and turn the region over to the buffalo. Roger Welsch calls the proposal "flapdoodle." My reaction is stronger—it's buffalo chip!

Setting aside for the moment all logical arguments against the proposal, but reserving the right to emotional outburst, my concern is that the Popper Plan would produce another disastrous situation—it would eliminate many great places to eat. Take, for example, the Market in Oshkosh. Its location in western Nebraska places it squarely in the middle of a buffalo wallow.

Since Oshkosh is a town of only 1057 people, I thought I'd have no trouble locating the Market. Wrong. I drove up and down the main street of town three times before I finally stopped at the drug store and asked for directions. "Only two buildings down from here," the clerk responded. I followed the directions, but they led me to a floral shop; no sign of a restaurant. I again asked directions and learned that only the front of the building was a floral shop. Once inside, it took the fragrance of fresh-baked bread to convince me I'd found the right spot.

A pleasant hostess greeted me and led me into the dining room past a Christmas party of twenty-one women. The atmosphere was that of a French country garden. The room was decorated with French country murals, flowers, and lattice work. A large tree with bare branches reaching to the ceiling stood in the center of the room. The tables were decorated as if for a party— red-and-green poinsettia tableclothes and floral centerpieces. The waitress asked if I'd ever had lunch with a room full of women as she handed me the menu filled with gourmet delights, including Crab Louie and a variety of quiches.

I started the meal with a hearty vegetable soup accompanied by a bowl of specially seasoned croutons. The ham-and-cheese quiche, garnished with attractively arranged fruit, was excellent, as was the warm homemade bread. I resisted the cheesecake and had a warm apple muffin for dessert. In the heart of the meat-and-potatoes country of the Sandhills, I was amazed to find this pocket of imaginative gourmet food, artfully presented. I relished it and thought again that the Market, like the whole area, is worth saving from the buffalo. Besides, real buffalo don't eat quiche.

The owner told me that she had been the cook for the previous owner who had started the restaurant several years before, but that restaurant had failed. The local bank took over the restaurant and, wanting to preserve it, asked her to run it for them. Before long she was able to convince the banker that she could not only cook, but could also manage a successful operation. She bought the building from the bank, and the business has thrived ever since. There was a sparkle in her eyes as she told me how much she enjoyed gourmet cooking and had plans for making the Market even better. She is a survivor.

As I walked out of the Market, a huge "V" of Canadian geese heading south honked overhead. The streets were busy, there were no empty storefronts, and the citizens spoke to me as I passed. I stopped and took a deep breath of the clear, crisp air. Then I turned and looked back down the wide main street toward the Market. I smiled to myself—not a buffalo in sight.

El Charrito—Scottsbluff

802 21st Avenue 308-32-3534

C hicago columnist Mike Royko, a man well-known for his strong opinions, doesn't mince words about nachos. "I'm convinced that those brave men died at the Alamo to prevent this dish from entering the United States." he writes. Well, I like nachos more than Mike, but I know what he's talking about when it comes to tracking down good, authentic Mexican food in the state of Nebraska. I skip the franchised conglomerates that serve food—ticorittos, chimichangas, texacos—that sound like an oil company or a South American dance.

For authentic Mexican food head west to Scottsbluff and the El Charrito. But don't expect pinatas and wide sombreros on the walls. The place looks like a mess hall at summer camp. And don't expect a strolling mariachi band; the only music I could detect was a rock-and-roll radio station blaring from a boom box in the kitchen. In fact, to get your food you have to get in line; there are no waiters or waitresses. You check in at the kitchen window when you think your food is ready. Atmosphere and service are not the main attractions.

El Charrito's strong point is the no-frills Mexican food, the kind they serve south of the border, and can describe only in Spanish. Fortunately for me, a local friend who could interpret the menu board accompanied me the evening I went. He said I couldn't go wrong if the dish contained the infamous green chile. My choice was three-alarm hot: it had rugged chunks of pork surrounded by those green chiles. In addition, the guacamole side dish was fresh with just the right blend of lemon and garlic, a cool counterpoint to the sizzling pork entree.

I should add that there are several similar cantinas in Scottsbluff. I recommend Rosita's for flautas and fajitas. Another one you might try is Pepe's where on Saturday nights, it's all-you-can-eat for $3.95.

18 West 17th, 308-632-3883

Mike and Mindy Jay are competitors. Mike, a former all-American high school football player and starting quarterback for Texas A & M's 1975 Southwest conference championship team, and Mindy, a master in western horsemanship, are testing their talents in a new arena. The Jays love to eat and cook so while living in Texas they started on the chili cookoff circuit. (A very big draw in Texas.) Mike reports, "Chili is the state dish. If you don't know how to cook chili in Texas, you're in pretty bad shape." After whetting their appetites (so to speak) on chili cookoffs, the pair expanded their repertoire to include barbecue, beans, and numerous other cookoffs.

How have they fared in their transition from physical to culinary competition? You guessed it. Champions again. They've won the Nebraska Chili Cookoff two years in a row, and have qualified three times for the World Championships.

Fans have urged these champion cooks to open a restaurant, and so in 1990, the Wildcat Eatery was born. Although it's still early in the game, the place seems like a winner.

Named after the scenic Wildcat Hills, the Eatery seats about 40 and is open only for lunch, except for the special Thursday supper feast. It specializes in a variety of deli sandwiches and offers an international special everyday, including exotic dishes like sesame and garlic flank steak, ratatouille, and stacked enchiladas with guacamole. Best of all, their menu includes championship barbecue, grilled Texas style over mesquite wood. It's truly a find in a state devoid of palatable barbecue. The Wildcat Eatery's "secret sauce," which the Jays claim as the world's greatest, is mild, sweet and delicious. Tabasco is available in case you want to heat it up a bit. The smoky flavor heightened by the delicate sauce is proof of why the Jays have dominated barbecue competition in the Midwest.

The highlight of week is Thursday evening at the Wildcat Eatery. On this night, the restaurant opens for a special all-you-can-eat barbecue and fixin's buffet for $6.99. The smoked meat selection includes chicken, brisket, ribs, and sausage. Folks in the Scottsbluff area have really taken to this food extravaganza. If you want great barbecue in enormous proportions, get there early; it's standing room only.

Try the Wildcat Eatery, the athletic Jay family will win you over.

Cowpoke Inn—Thedford

308-645-2253

The Sandhills are the heart of cowboy country and Thedford's Cowpoke Inn is in the heart of the Sandhills. Like the Hyannis Hotel Bar, the walls of the Cowpoke Inn are decorated with photographs of local cowboys bulldogging steers, roping calves, and riding broncs and bulls.

During the noon hour the place is loaded with ranchers and ranch hands wearing cowboy hats and boots and speaking in a tongue foreign to city folk. You'll hear talk of cattle futures, weaning weights, embryo transplants, expected progeny differences, Charolais crossbreds, artificial insemination, fixin' fence, and unending speculation about rain. There's plenty of local color in this personality parade straight out of a western movie. The faces are creased and sun-leathered, the smiles easy, and the laughter uninhibited.

As in most Sandhills cafes, beef is king. At lunch, it's strictly cowboy cuisine—roast beef or burgers made from one hundred percent ground beef. At dinner, it's prime rib or steaks. The portions are generous, and it's easy to overeat (there's a cowboy saying that if you walk out of a cafe after a huge meal half-way between "My God!" and "Oh Lord," you "overdone" it). Also, the prices seem immune to inflation.

If you're not hungry when you hit Thedford, too bad. Stop in anyway. It's one of the few places around (besides Mines Drug in Hooper) where you can still get a five-cent cup of coffee. That's a rare enough fact for Paul Harvey to announce on his radio show!

NORTH CENTRAL REGION

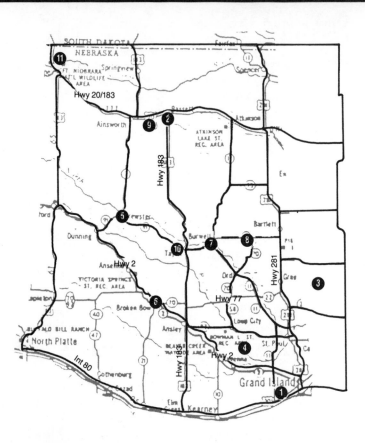

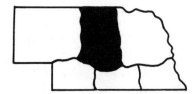

North Central

1. Alda—Dowd's
2. Bassett—Range Cafe
3. Belgrade—Silverjack Saloon
4. Boelus—The Golden Nugget
5. Brewster—Doc Middleton's Bar and Cafe
6. Broken Bow—The Lobby
7. Burwell—Buck's Bakery
8. Ericson—Hungry Horse Saloon
9. Long Pine—Hidden Paradise
10. Taylor—The Bridge Club
11. Valentine—The Peppermill

Silverjack Saloon—Belgrade

308-357-9801

There's always something going on at the Silverjack Saloon. On Saturday night the crowd at the Saloon nearly doubles the population of Belgrade. Once a month you can dance to such memorables as the Knights of the turntable. Owners Jack and Debbie Nelson also stir things up with basketball, pool, or hula hoop contests. If it's fun, they do it at the Silverjack.

The saloon occupies an eighty-five-year-old brick building, once home to a feed store and grocery before settling into its role as an eating and drinking establishment. The Nelsons have taken an extra step in decorating their saloon. They painted the classy, pressed-tin ceiling, stripped the plaster, installed barn siding, and covered the walls with antiques. Jack's antique pedal toys and tin signs are everywhere. Wherever she could find the space, Debbie filled in with her collection of tin containers and bric-a-brac. Look carefully and you'll even find a Sonja Henie calendar.

And food is part of the attraction at the Silverjack too. Debbie is an excellent cook. She packs them in on Thursday nights for her Mexican specials, and on Sundays there is a popular buffet served in the parlor adjoining the main room. The regular menu is also pretty good. It includes a pound-plus steak, the half-pound Silverjack Burger, and my favorite, the Winchester—a chicken fried steak topped with melted cheese, lettuce, tomato, and pickle on a hoagie bun. (Incidentally, central Nebraska from Palmer to Belgrade to Taylor is the happy hunting ground for those who pursue the elusive chicken fried steak.)

Fun and games, friendly people, antiques, and good food. You'll find them all at the Silverjack Saloon.

308-996-9260

Roger Welsch, Nebraska folklorist and recent TV celebrity, claims, "The Golden Nugget in Boelus on any Saturday night is the greatest steakhouse in America, make that in the world." His choice for second best? "The Golden Nugget on Friday night." Welsch made these statements the night he was unanimously elected president of the National Liars' Hall of Fame in nearby Dannebrog. If pressed, he will back down a bit by saying the Nugget's at least one of the seven or eight best places to eat in Howard County and most certainly the best place in Boelus.

Perhaps he's right. At least the townspeople think a lot of the place. The city fathers have constructed a large sign on the edge of town: "Home of Famous Ball Teams and the Golden Nugget Visited by Famous People." The famous people are perhaps Welsch and Charles Kuralt, who periodically stops in at the Nugget when doing pieces for his CBS-TV series.

Where is Boelus? Well, it's four miles south of Nysted, about three miles north of St. Michael, or ten miles southwest of Rockville. Give up? It's twenty-five miles northwest of Grand Island. The community of 189 also boasts a grocery store, a gas station, and the Boelus State Bank.

The August evening I was in Boelus, it was 101 degrees outside. But inside the Nugget it was cold enough to hang beef and dark enough to pass for a romantic rendezvous in some big-city bistro. When my eyes adjusted to the abrupt change in light, I recognized the Nebraska steakhouse surroundings complete with the hallmark of Nebraska restaurants, the ever-present collection. The Nugget's collection is of liquor bottles, all shapes and sizes assembled along the walls above the booths.

One glance at the menu confirmed that I was out of the high-rent district—the most expensive steak was $7.00. It was better than most steaks that sell for twice as much. The hash browns were crisp not dry, golden brown, not greasy. Welsch may be an honest man after all, but don't let that get around. He might lose his place in the Liars' Hall of Fame.

The owners of the Nugget, Dick and Beth Whitefoot, moved from Fremont twenty-nine years ago. Beth does most of the cooking, and Dick runs the bar, keeping everyone entertained with a vast array of Boelus gossip. He occasionally joins a customer in one of the state's favorite cocktails, red beer (beer and tomato juice, to non-Nebraskans).

"When we first started out hamburgers were only twenty-five cents and the Saturday night special was a dollar T-bone," Dick says. "I made more money off of those prices than I do now." Despite its remote location, the business has continued to grow. The Whitefoots have made two additions to the building, and it's still filled on most weekends. Dick estimates they sell about 400 steaks a night, but adds, "We just wanted to get into business. We had no aspirations for a place this size. It just gets bigger and bigger."

If you're ever within fifty miles of Boelus on a Saturday night, drive to the Nugget. The gas will cost you a little extra, but you'll make it back on the price of the meal. Who knows, you might run into a celebrity. And, Welsch says to arrive early because you may have to park several blocks away, and the whole town has only two blocks.

Doc Middleton

An Essay

Steal a few horses, shoot a few hombres, break out of jail, and do a little bootlegging. Who knows, maybe you'll be famous. Maybe they'll even name a restaurant after you. That's what happened to James Riley, alias Doc Middleton, one of Nebraska's most famous outlaws. The citizens of Brewster, memorializing the feats of one of their former residents, named their only restaurant, a steakhouse and saloon, in his honor. It's located across the street from the saloon and gambling hall Doc operated in the late 1870s. When I ate at Doc Middleton's recently, I learned more about this fabled outlaw.

Doc is described as a notorious thug, gambler, murderer, and the "King of Horse Thieves." A one-time deputy sheriff, he was generous with his money and maintained a good relationship with the ranchers in the Sandhills. These ranchers referred to him as the "unwickedest outlaw," a "Robin Hood-style robber." Some have gone so far as to say he was "always a gentleman" (granted, there were some narrow-minded folk who considered it ungentlemanly for him to shoot at them or swipe their horses). However, Doc lived by his own set of principles: he never shot a man in the back, buried all the men he killed (if his getaway schedule permitted), visited his wife at least twice a year, usually bathed on Saturday nights, didn't belch in church, and paid for his dinner before he stole your horse.

> Doc lived by his own set of principles: he never shot a man in the back, buried all the men he killed, visited his wife at least twice a year, usually bathed on Saturday nights, didn't belch in church, and paid for his dinner before he stole your horse.

He killed several men in Texas and Kansas and was wanted by the Texas Rangers for horse stealing, a crime Texans equated with murder. Doc, however, considered himself merely a "dealer in stock." Whatever he was, he was colorful.

Upon his arrival in Nebraska in the 1870s, Doc continued to covet the other fella's horse. He once stole thirty-four horses, then was captured and held in the Sidney jail. Doc simply tunneled his way out and made his getaway, on a stolen horse, of course.

Many of his escapes were attributed to the fact that he got on well with Sandhills ranchers. On one occasion, Doc was chased by a posse from Ogallala to Sidney. Bystanders describe him spurring his horse across a bridge near Bridgeport, reins in his teeth and guns blazing in the night. Taking refuge with a friendly rancher, he traded his horse for a fresh one and escaped.

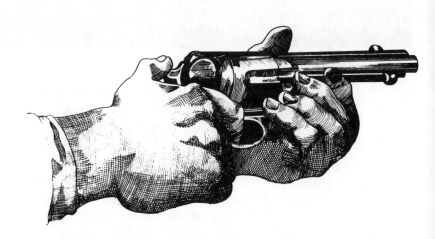

Ranging far and wide through the Sandhills, Doc Middleton led the Pony Gang, including such outlaws as Black Jack Nolan, Limber Dick, Black Bill, Count Shevaloff, Little Joe Johnson, Gold Tooth Jack, Curly Grimes, Luke Short, and Kid Wade. But the law finally caught up with him. In 1879, he started a five-year term in the penitentiary in Lincoln (for horse theft). Upon release he did some cowboying, rode in a cross-country horse race from Chadron to Chicago in 1893, and worked in Buffalo Bill's Wild West Show. In 1887, he opened the saloon on the east side of the main street in Brewster. In his retirement years, he also owned saloons in Gordon and Bassett. He died in 1913 in the county jail of Douglas, Wyoming, where he was serving a sentence for bootlegging, a curious end for a man who didn't drink.

Doc Middleton's—Brewster

308-547-2215

By the summer of 1986, the town of Brewster had all but disappeared. The steakhouse/bar, garage, and grocery store had closed. Six stores on Brewster's wide main street stood empty. Only a two-story green court-house, the tallest building in town, and the post office kept the town alive. Standing outside the court-house at the end of Lincoln Avenue, there was nothing to see except empty stores and the Sandhills beyond.

The loss of the steakhouse/bar seemed to pain the twenty-three residents of the village more than the loss of the other businesses. It also left the surrounding

ranchers "out there in the hills living by themselves."
County Clerk Edna Spencer described the feeling of
loss by saying, "We don't have anyplace where we can
share anymore." County Attorney Joe Divis, a resident
for thirty-nine years, put it a little stronger, "It'd be nice
to have a tavern where you could sit around and bitch."

But the people of Brewster didn't just sit around.
Three local young men decided to start a new steakhouse and bar, and community members donated their
evenings to remodel the former grocery store. They
called it Doc Middleton's in honor of the friendly outlaw who had operated a bar in Brewster in the late
1880s.

The food is plain ranch cooking, honest western
food. Saturday's prime rib is their best offering and the
pies are all made from scratch. It won't make the auto-
club travel guide, but the food, the history and the
town spirit make it a worth-while stop for lovers of
Nebraska.

Like ole Doc, the folks are mannerly, but unlike
him, they won't steal your horse.

The Lobby Restaurant—Broken Bow

509 South 9th, 308-871-3363

H ungry for something other than steakhouse fare?
Longing for the exotic taste of orange roughy,
oriental prawns, mandarin plum chicken, red snapper,
scampi, steak oscar, or blackened swordfish? Most folks
would tell you to head for the big city lights of Lincoln,
Omaha, or Denver. Not me. There's a place between

Lincoln and Denver where you can get all of these things, plus great beef. And at prices substantially lower due to the low, small-town overhead. Interested? Then head for the heart of beef country—the Sandhills; head to a renovated old hotel in a small town—the Arrow in Broken Bow; head to one of the best dang restaurants in rural Nebraska—the Lobby Restaurant.

The Arrow Hotel, built back in 1928 in the Plains style of architecture, has always had a thriving restaurant, except for a few years in the early 80s when the hotel and restaurant were renovated by an enterprising group of Broken Bow investors. The hotel reopened in 1984 with "luxury suites" on the second and third floors. The restaurant re-opened in 1986.

The restaurant's decor is a cross between antique and art deco. The dining booths are constructed from old doors of the rooms upstairs, with their numbers still intact. Katherine and I dined between rooms 133 and 137 the night we went there. Art deco wall fixtures dramatically cast light up and down the dark lacquered walls creating shadows and the atmosphere of a Chicago speakeasy in the 20s. The tables are formal and immaculate with burgundy and gray linen. It's a quiet, comfortable atmosphere, refreshing after the haphazard ambience of traditional Nebraska steakhouses.

From the wide variety on the menu, we selected mandarin plum chicken and pepper steak. The chicken was covered with a sweet plum sauce and the steak tender and spicy in a dark wine sauce; both were excellent choices. With our entrees, there were the kinds of extras that set apart outstanding restaurants: homemade rolls, instead of dry bakery ones; a relish tray with dip; a crisp green salad with a house dressing that included capers and big chunks of blue cheese;

black bean soup; and baked potato or rice pilaf. There was even herbal tea.

We envision a fun spring weekend in Broken Bow to include checking into a suite at the Arrow Hotel, riding our bicycles on one of the 20-mile bike tour loops in the area (wide shoulders, little traffic, historical sites, and fabulous scenery), sampling some more of the Lobby's goodies, and going to the quarter-horse races at the county fairgrounds on Friday or Saturday night. It'll match a weekend in Denver for luxury, cosmopolitan dining, recreation, history, scenery, and exercise, and certainly beat the price.

Buck's Bakery—Burwell

141 Grand Avenue, 308-346-4589

The motel alarm went off at 5 a.m., an ungodly hour, especially because I'd arrived in Burwell quite late the night before, the last customer to check in the motel. It was snowing and the temperature was in the low teens, both inside and out. I rolled over, pulled up the blankets, and hoped it was all a bad dream. I don't wake up easily.

For me, waking up is like evolution. At first, I'm stuck in bed, (a fish lolling on the bottom). When I get the strength to move, I slither out of bed like a reptile. It's at least noon before I walk upright. After three cups of coffee, I get language. Somehow, that morning I had to be on the road and in Lincoln by early afternoon. Instinct pointed me in one direction—I had to find someplace that had lots of coffee and some food.

This survival instinct put me in the car and sent me toward downtown Burwell. I managed to find the one spot with lights on and stumbled in the door. It was bright inside and very warm. Despite my semi-conscious state, I recognized the aroma of freshly brewed coffee mixed with the comforting smell of fresh-baked rolls, donuts, and breads.

After three cups of coffee, sure enough, the world came into focus. Serving me was owner, Buck Newberry, a retired Marine Corps sergeant who has been

Rodeo Entrance
Burwell

waking up Burwell with strong coffee, great baked goods, and hearty conversation for the past twenty-six years. Buck is not only the three-time mayor of Burwell, but he is also one of the area's experts on cowboy history.

After downing my fourth cup of coffee and third hot-from-the-oven Danish, I remember Buck telling me that his building was probably the oldest one still in use in Burwell. Originally, it was used for medicine shows. The best medicine for me that morning was Buck's coffee and rolls.

As I drove home to Lincoln, I vowed to go back to Buck's Bakery for lunch sometime after a full night's sleep. I am curious to find what bits of history I missed before the coffee activated my brain. Besides, the rumor is that Buck's lunches are every bit as therapeutic as his coffee and rolls.

Hungry Horse Saloon—Ericson

308-653-5111

The main street of Ericson is a scene right out of the movie "High Noon"—a wide, dirt street; a place to tie your horse; and a wooden sidewalk. What's missing is Gary Cooper, Grace Kelly, and a gunfight.

But what really steals the scene is an authentic western tavern, the Hungry Horse Saloon. The Hungry Horse's battered frame building looks like it needs horses out front instead of the row of pickups. Like most antiques, it could use some sprucin' up, but I think it looks better with its decades-old patina. Evidently some of the locals disagree: As I stood in the middle of the street to take a picture of the Hungry Horse, a cowgirl in a yellow pickup stopped and suggested that I wait until they paint the place. That'll be a long wait.

Perched up on the eaves of the saloon, looking like a cowboy parked it up there on a Saturday night, is an old wagon, or what's left of it. (I take it as a sign that some good times have been had in this town.)

The saloon's interior has rough wood paneling, a bruised linoleum floor, and the brands of local ranchers burned into the walls. The bar and dance floor are separated by a long strand of workhorse fly harness. On the other side of the bar is the dining room. Thursdays through Saturdays it serves Nebraska steakhouse fare. What more can I say?

Food and drink are available at the Hungry Horse, of course, but fun is the bar's top draw. The saloon sponsors unusual events, like a pasture golf tournament. The well-oiled teams rocket their balls toward links located not only in surrounding pastures but throughout the town as well. Photos of last year's champions show a happy foursome sporting long, baggy shorts, cowboy boots, Hawaiian shirts, fluorescent sunglasses, and Resitols, with favorite beverages held high.

Even bigger than pasture golf is the Sandhills Turtle Race which has been held in early August for the past sixteen years. You can bring your own turtle or rent one on the spot. Take a look at some of the race rules:

No lead ropes, probes, whips, or mechanical devices permitted. (Mechanical devices were banned when a contestant inserted a remote control device in an empty turtle shell to wipe out the competition.)

No starting blocks.

No coaching.

Claws cannot be sharpened, nor may shells be greased.

Time limit for each race—across the finish or 15 minutes, whichever occurs first.

No steroids.

Don't laugh. Turtle races are becoming one of this country's newest spectator sports. For raw speed, thrills, and awesome competition, there's nothing better than the Sandhills Turtle Races at the Hungry Horse.

The Nebraska Games

An Essay

C harlie Bowlus and Hubbard Renfro are middle-aged, good 'ole boys who, like many Nebraska men, love competition, any competition. Charlie is short and stocky, stubborn enough to cling to his high-school crew-cut. A dogged competitor, he plays every game, whatever the game, like he was fighting a holy war. In high school he broke the little finger on his right hand in the first football game of his senior year. Afraid the doc would put a cast on it and bench him, he said nothing and played his entire senior year, through football, basketball, and track, without anyone noticing. When the doctor finally discovered it the following summer, the finger had frozen into a curl. (You should have seen the trouble he got into at the University for his disrespectful salutes to ROTC superiors). Hub is six feet four, and has shoulders like a huge coat hanger. He's still slender, except for a slight paunch above his belt, with abrupt features—a lantern jaw, dark brown eyes, thick silver-gray hair, and a smile so wide you can count his

> Charlie Bowlus and Hubbard Renfro are middle-aged, good 'ole boys who love competition, any competition.

back molars. Like the hub of a wheel, he's solid. Although he talks less than Charlie, and sometimes appears lethargic, inside there's the tenacity of a fighter who won't go down no matter how long you pound on him.

Like Charlie, Hub lives and loves sports. He once took off all alone and drove clear to Baton Rouge, Louisiana, because he'd heard the Husker-LSU football game would only be televised in Louisiana. When he arrived, they told him he'd been misinformed by his Yankee friends. "Sorry Cornshucker, the game ain't on TV. Besides," they said, "them Cornshuckers is jus' gonna be Tiger meat." The stadium was sold out, so Hub sat hunched on a stool at the Bayou Bengal Bar just across the street. He drank Louisiana beer, ate Cajun ribs, and listened to the game on the radio. Periodically he went to the door to hear the roar of the crowd and stare longingly at the stadium.

These two old buddies grew up together in a small north central Nebraska town, played on the same peewee ball team, and eventually went to Lincoln together to play in the 1957 class D basketball tournament. The Wildcats won state their senior year, but haven't been back to the tournament since. The locals still talk about that Wildcat team, and former coach Arnold Grundorf says, "It was the best darn team I ever coached, and Hub at forward and Charlie at point were my best boys."

Hub and Charlie returned to their hometown after college. Hub's the only lawyer in town ("That's one too many," Charlie says). Charlie teaches history and coaches the track team ("How can you coach kids to run fast when you never learned yourself?" Hub asks).

At the tavern one Friday night over beer and catfish, Hub and Charlie argued, as they often did, about which of them was the best athlete. Hub, more talkative than usual, said, "When the chips were down in the state finals, I tossed in twenty-seven points." Charlie retorted, "That's because you shot the ball every time you touched it. You're the Will Rogers of basketball; you never saw a shot you didn't like."

"Sour grapes, Charlie," Hub replied. "You couldn't shoot. That's why they called you a defensive specialist." The argument grew louder and hotter. Finally, their wives Angie and Shellie suggested that they settle it once and for all with their own version of the Cornhusker Games. Another debate followed about what events to include. Charlie's wife Angie settled it: "We'll pick the events," she said.

Hub and Charlie presumed they would choose events like free throw shooting, swimming, or putting. But the women had a different idea. They liked to poke around in small-town antique shops and sample country-cafe cooking, and figured they would use this competitive fervor to get their husbands to take them on excursions where they could do just that. So to determine the champion, the women selected seven events on seven summer weekends in seven different small towns.

The competition began at the Lewis and Clark Dairy Expo in Crofton. The first event was the cow-chip flip. Angie and Shellie watched impatiently as the boys warmed up. "Watch my discus form, Honey," Hub yelled as he let fly with a warmup heave that shattered upon release. With that, Shellie and Angie turned in unison and headed toward the nearest antique shop. But Hub won the chip flip. (Charlie's toss went off the side of his hand, was caught by a strong cross wind, and sent a small group of spectators scurrying.) Hub also turned in a "moooving" performance in the cow-milking contest so when the events were tallied at the end of the day, Hub had won the Dairy Expo event.

Tired and sore, Hub and Charlie walked slowly back to the car to meet Shellie and Angie. They opened the trunk to stow their gear, and found it full of antiques. They topped off the day with steaks at Bogner's. For these two Nebraska jocks the day had not only been tiring, it had also been expensive.

The next week the action shifted to Eustis for the annual Biffy Grand Prix. The privies, hauled to Eustis in Hub's sparetire-less horse trailer, were built to Grand Prix specifications. Required to resemble a traditional outhouse mounted on wheels, they had to be four feet by four feet with a quarter moon cut in the door and entries could be either one-or-two-seaters. One passenger, Shellie or Angie in this case, had to ride inside the building wearing a helmet and seat belt. Hub and Charlie were to push the privies along the race course.

> The next week the action shifted to Eustis for the annual Biffy Grand Prix.

Charlie evened the score with a victory in this event after Hub went around a corner too fast and dumped the vehicle and Shellie in a ditch on the outskirts of town. When he finally pulled her out of the crashed vehicle, she gave him a verbal thrashing that drew a round of applause from a group of spectators watching from a front yard. (When Charlie heard about the crash, he told Hub that his performance "stunk.") Shellie threatened to find a good lawyer and sue Hub for whiplash.After some difficult negotiations, Hub was able to settle her case by agreeing to take everyone to the Pool Hall for Mexican food.

The third event of the Games was held at the Wayne Chicken Show, a celebration of the chicken including a free feed with omelets and barbecued chicken, a chicken parade, and the crowning of Chicken a la King. The show also featured many games of skill, including an egg toss, a rooster-crowing contest (won by an English silver duck rooster with forty-one crowing outbursts in thirty minutes), and a chicken "cluck off" in which the entrants imitate the sound of a laying hen. Joel Vavra of Crete clucked his way to his third straight title, although he was pushed by Bill Patrick of Saginaw, Michigan, who entered after Vavra accused him of being too chicken to give it a try.

The event selected for Hub and Charlie was the chicken-flying contest. In this event, a large rural mailbox with front and back doors is mounted on a pole about ten feet above the ground. A contestant climbs a ladder to the mailbox, inserts a live chicken in the back door, and, at the sound of a whistle, opens the front door. The chicken that flies farthest is declared the winner.

Hub borrowed one of Wilbur Gomarth's Rhode Island Reds with Wilbur's assurances that this "superhen" would "fly like an eagle." Charlie, on the other hand, was very secretive about his entry, kept in a black box with holes so small that no one could see in.

Hub went first, climbed the ladder, inserted the chicken, and, at the signal jerked open the front door of the box. For the first few seconds the hen only poked out her head. Patiently, Hub coaxed her with a gentle clucking sound. Finally, she moved to the edge of the box, but hesitated again, hunkering down like a kid reluctant to make her first dive off the high board. Hub, with patience exhausted, goosed his entry. She flapped her wings, but dropped like a stone. The judges generously recorded her flight as two feet.

By the time Charlie mounted the ladder, the leading chicken had a recorded flight of twenty-one feet. Charlie opened the door to his mysterious box so that no one could see his bird crawl into the mailbox. When the whistle sounded, a strange-looking chicken with a long tail exploded out of the mailbox. The crowd gasped as the bird soared to the end of the block, circled the bakery, banked to the left at the drug store, and disappeared from sight. Hub hollered "Foul!" and the judges disqualified Charlie for his illegal entry. They seemed to think Charlie's chicken was a ring-necked pheasant.

Before they headed home, the couples drove to the Hotel in Wakefield. Hub ordered fried chicken to celebrate.

... seventeen entrants were given free beer, blank paper, a pen, and one hour to compose a country-western song.

Throughout the summer the competition stayed close. Charlie won the Avoca Quackoff goose races. (Hub's goose laid an egg at the starting line and never moved off the mark.) Hub won the Sargent Chokecherry Jamboree pit spit. Charlie got nervous and suffered from "cotton mouth": the pit stuck to his tongue and he almost choked. (Hub had no problem with his pit and let fly with a splendid twelve-footer.) Charlie won the Sandhills Turtle Races, sponsored by the Hungry Horse Saloon in Ericson. (Hub's turtle, Whirl-A-Way, pulled a hamstring during warmups and had to be scratched.)

By the end of the summer, The score was tied at three to three. For the last event the women decided that the boys needed some intellectual stimulation so they chose a country-western song-writing contest in northwestern Nebraska for the final event. (The women neglected to tell the boys that their decision had been influenced by a great antique shop in Chadron and the prospect of dinner at O'Doherty's in Crawford.)

At this event, held in the only tavern in a town of 173, seventeen entrants were given free beer, blank paper, a pen, and one hour to compose a country-western song.

Hub had writer's block, but won the prize for the most beer consumed. Charlie, however, won third place in the "sentimental-romantic" category, clinching his victory in the competition with Hub. His prize-winning entry, nasally monotoned to the tune of "You're So Sweet, Horseflies Keep Hanging Round Your Face," went like this:

LORD, THERE'S A LOT OF YOU, BABY

Just can't forget the first time we met
in the hog-sortin pens at the Knox County
Fair.
You was plumb up to your thighs,
when I peered into them eyes,
Crossed they was, but honey I just don't care.

You're really nifty.
You weigh two-fifty?
Do love your hair; it's everywhere.

If arms could reach round your torso,
You bet I'd do so.
They'd play our tune—Schlitz For Two,
And I'd waltz clean 'cross Nebraska with you.

(Chorus)
Lord, there's a lot of you baby!
Good thing.
'Cuz I just can't git enuf.

Darlin', wanted to give you diamond and
pearls,
But I'm short this week,
so this here's my heart.

Years rolled by—you got plain and old,
Still I tell the world,
with a voice loud and bold,
She smells a bit,
but has a heart of gold.

So the competition ended—but not the competi-
tiveness. Hub demanded a rematch.

Significant Others—North Central

Dowds —Alda
308-382-4837

Operated by a branch of the Dowd family
tree of Dreisbach's fame (Grand Island).
Dowds know how to serve great beef. Go for
the big Sunday brunch.

Range Cafe—Bassett
402-684-3379

Old West ambiance in a real cattlemen's cafe
and hotel (built by local ranchers to put up
cattle buyers). Noted for excellent beef,
homemade pie, and unbelievably low prices.
Be careful, these ranchers are great salesmen;
you might walk out owning a herd.

Hidden Paradise—Long Pine
402-273-4144

I've heard this Long Pine restaurant is a heavenly place to eat. That may be, but when I looked for the Hidden Paradise, I couldn't find it.

The Bridge Club—Taylor
308-942-9816

Don't plan on playing cards. This is a club for serious eaters only (Bridge is a family name). Famous for chicken-fried steak, some say the best in Nebraska. Filling luncheon specials include huge hot beef sandwiches and salad bar for $4.95. Marilyn Goble's sour cream raisin pie sells out early. For local color and a chance to catch up on farm and ranch news, sit in at the long coffee table.

The Pepper Mill —Valentine
402-376-1440

Homemade chow in a newly remodeled setting in cowboy country. Excellent beef, but also lobster, frog legs, and scampi. Luncheon specials vary. The Pepper Mill is nothing to sneeze at. Fun beer garden in summer.

NORTHEAST REGION

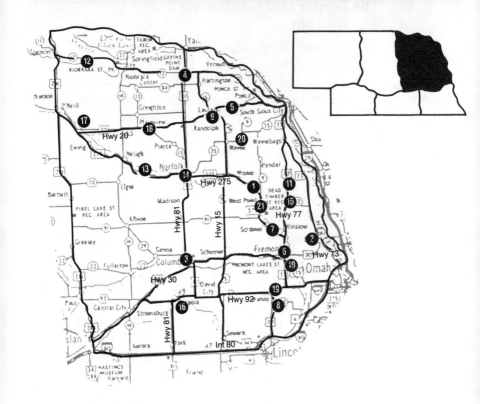

Northeast

1. Beemer—Marilyn's Tea Room
2. Blair—Cafe on Main
3. Columbus—Glur's Tavern
   Muffin Shoppe
4. Crofton—Bogner's
5. Dixon—Euni's Place
6. Fremont—Fremont Dinner Train
7. Hooper—Mine's Drug
   The Office Bar and Grill
8. Ithaca—Elsie's Cafe
9. Laurel—Wagon Wheel
10. Leshara—Longbranch

11. Lyons Bakery and Cafe
12. Lynch—Bakery Cafe
13. Meadow Grove—Sportsman's Bar and Grill
14. Norfolk—The Uptown Eating Establishment
15. Oakland—Corner Cafe Coffee Shop
16. Osceola—Ye Ole Mill
17. Page—Beef 'n Stuff
18. Plainview—The Headquarters
19. Wahoo—Fairview Cafe
    OK Market
20. Wakefield—Hotel Wakefield
21. West Point—Neligh House

Marilyn's Tea Room—Beemer

417 East 3rd Street, 402-528-3282

"L ittle Things Mean a Lot" was the title of a popular song in the fifties. That title would be an appropriate slogan for Marilyn's Tea Room in Beemer. At Marilyn's, everything—even little things like the soda crackers—is homemade. No, I'm not kidding, no Nabisco saltines, no pre-prepared frozen food, no potatoes out of a box, no rolls from the local bakery truck, and above all, no "brung-in" pies.

Marilyn Schantz is the owner, manager, waitress and gourmet cook at Marilyn's. Since she does all the cooking, with the help of her mother, the fare is consistently good. The regular luncheon menu (she only serves lunch, but is open in the evening by appointment) includes chicken crepes, cornish game hen, Windsor pork chops, family-style baked ham and chicken, and daily specials. A vegetable sandwich topped with poppy seed dressing is also a very popular item.

After a bountiful bowl of old-fashioned vegetable soup accompanied by the made-from-scratch soda crackers, I tried the chicken crepes, which were fabulous. The rolls—too often a near-miss in so-called better restaurants—were moist and warm, homemade with a tender light brown crust. The food was not only very tasty; it was presented in an artful way. The entree was like a picture out of *Gourmet* magazine. The delicate crepes, arranged on a bed of leaf lettuce, were filled with tender slices of chicken and topped with a light cream sauce sprinkled with almond slivers. A sprig of grapes and an orange slice on the side made an appealing plate of yellow, red, green, and orange that looked almost too beautiful to eat. As Julia Child would say, "The food was so beautifully arranged on the plate you know someone's fingers have been all over it." I topped lunch off with coconut pie that was fit for the gods.

Plenty more little things delight diners at Marilyn's. The place itself is charming. It's located in a hundred-year-old Queen-Anne-style house on a corner lot surrounded by cottonwoods. The white house was built by town founder A.D. Beemer in 1886. The restaurant and a quilt shop occupy the first floor and Marilyn lives upstairs; she had run an eighteen-bed nursing home there before starting the Tea Room.

The interior features lots of woodwork and is filled with cleverly-arranged "garage sale junk," as Marilyn calls it. Neither the furniture nor the china match, adding charm and creating a very homey, comfortable atmosphere, the kind that reminds you of Grandma's house at Thanksgiving, when mismatched tables for all the guests filled the living room because she didn't have a dining-room table big enough for everybody. The chilly winter day I was in Beemer, I dined in the south room with dark blue, calico-print wallpaper and abundant windows which allowed sunlight to stream in through lace curtains, and made the room even cozier.

The clientele at Marilyn's was interesting as well. There were well-dressed ladies, businessmen, and farmers in bib overalls, proof that you don't have to own a steakhouse to attract the whole range of Nebraska appetites.

As you can tell, I fell in love with Marilyn's. It is one of Nebraska's hidden treasures. It's a little place, in a little town, where little things count. And in my way of thinking, nothing is more important.

2301 11th Street, 402-564-8615

W hen you walk into Glur's Tavern, you naturally catch a light, sudsy whiff of beer blended with grilling burgers, but take a deeper breath. There's another smell at Glur's—an antique smell that comes with history.

Glur's Tavern
Columbus

Glur's is the oldest continuously operated tavern west of the Missouri River. Back in 1876, two Swiss immigrant brothers, Joseph and William Bucher, built what was then called The Bucher Saloon. An early helper in the saloon was the young Louis Glur who in 1914 purchased it. He and his family operated it up until a few years ago when it was sold to the present owners.

If the creaking wooden floor could talk, it would tell about a day in the 1880s when Buffalo Bill stomped in and offered to buy a full round of drinks. When he put a $1000 bill on the bar to pay for the round, Joe Bucher fainted dead away at the thought of having to make change.

The floor would also tell how Glur's was not a popular place with the womenfolk. Indoor plumbing wasn't installed until the 1960s, and the ladies didn't care to use the privies out back. Louis Glur couldn't understand why. "Always kept the path to the privies shoveled in the winter," he used to say.

The two-story building is located on the edge of downtown Columbus. The spacious bar and dining area are filled with old wooden tables and chairs and usually with locals busily chowing down on traditional American grub—soup and burgers. A picture of John Wayne and a certificate attesting to Glur's status as the oldest tavern in the west hang on plain walls. One unique newer feature is the recreation area in the back. In warm weather the area is filled with families enjoying the beer garden atmosphere, playing or watching others play basketball, volleyball, or horseshoes.

Glur's is listed in the National Register of Historic Places, and it continues a long tradition of treating its customers well and seeing to it that they have a good time. Here's hoping it's around a hundred years from now.

The Universal Steakhouse

When you think of it, most Nebraska steakhouses are pretty much the same: from the outside (Morton steel) to the inside (dark with electric beer signs), down to the menu (prime rib on Saturdays), the perfume of charring beef, and the five-cent mints. Ross's in Omaha, Dreisbach's in Grand Island, Butch's Bar in Hershey: a franchiser couldn't ask for a better formula.

Their buildings are mere children, twenty-five years old or younger, no old houses or converted department stores. Many resemble metal hog-confinement houses. Sometimes they're spiffed up a bit with some fake rock, weathered barn siding, or a brick facade, but landscaping is conspicuously absent. Usually the sign out front is the most distinguishing feature.

Inside, they're undistinguished, usually with low, flat ceilings. The walls range from knotty pine paneling to painted drywall and are often half-heartedly covered with western relics—wooden cooking utensils, mis-matched spurs, a Russell print of a cowboy roping a steer, a branding iron, scenes painted on buck saws, and maybe a framed set of 12-inch barbed wire. Special touches are the wagon wheel light fixtures or local brands burned into the walls. Some ambitious places in consultation with restaurant decorators (who think art deco is the Greek kid who lived around the corner) have adopted the cluttered look, known as flea-market-on-the wall. And you'll also see red-flocked wallpaper reminiscent of a cattle baron's game room or a bordello.

> . . . most Nebraska steakhouses are pretty much the same. . .

Usually the fixtures consist of formica tables set with paper or plastic placemats and paper napkins. The chairs are durable metal, the booths black or brown naugahyde speckled with burns from cigarettes that missed the black plastic ashtrays. The lighting is dim at best, unless the beer signs have spilled over from the bar.

The menus are honest and plain, either wrinkled and grease-stained or enclosed in battle-scarred plastic to prevent such mishaps. No tricky foreign dishes here, no table-side flambes, no steak tartare. You will find chopped sirloin, filet mignon, club, T-bone, sirloin, New York strip, and token offerings of fish or chicken, usually frozen, then batter-fried.

Steakhouse meals include a trip to a salad bar (the trend is toward volume and infinite variety), or else a bowl of iceberg lettuce with a revolving stainless-steel dressing caddy. The steaks are always accompanied by potatoes—hash browns, baked, American fries, french fries, etc. (Nebraska and Idaho must have some kind of trade agreement that keeps all other vegetables from crossing our borders.) I can't remember eating green beans, corn, broccoli, or peas with steakhouse fare.

> One of the best steaks I ever had was at a tiny saloon, where my filet cost only $5.95.

The prices are unbelievably low. I've had great steaks all over the state for under $8. One of the best steaks I ever had was at a tiny saloon, then called the Sport and Go Cafe, where my filet cost only $5.95. I don't think I've ever paid more than $15 for a Nebraska steak. In New York City the tag would be $30, in Tokyo, as much as $150.

It's downright monotonous—wherever you go in this state, you'll find an otherwise unremarkable local steakhouse serving, at a good price, the best beef in

America, which, of course, is the best beef in the world. And that's something even an accomplished franchiser can't touch.

Bogner's Steak House—Crofton

402-388-4626

You remember the ill-fated Devil's Nest project located north of Crofton on Lewis and Clark Lake? It was going to be the biggest resort in the Midwest. The reasons for its failure are many, but some blame its demise on location—too far away from the area's big population centers. How, then, do we explain the success of one of Nebraska's largest and best-known steakhouses—Bogner's in Crofton?

The answer: success can follow despite poor location if you give the customers what they want—and what they want in a restaurant is consistently good food.

Both the restaurant and its present owner began their careers at the bottom. Forty years ago Bogner's was a small-town cafe reclaimed from the ruins of an abandoned gas station. Now, addition after addition attest to its popularity. Tom Pavlik, one of a line of successful owners of Bogner's, started his restaurant career as a dishwasher in Norfolk. Now he is not only a part-owner of Bogner's, but also of the Wagon Wheel in Laurel and Becker's in Norfolk.

The menu has amazing variety: crablegs; flamed escargot; tender, sizzling Nebraska steaks. The problem is that before you get to the entrees, you have to go through a salad bar with as many different dishes as Las Vegas has casinos (I had counted thirty when I gave up). If the plate had been a truck, I'd have been cited for a load violation.

The food is so good that folks drive there from miles away. On almost any night, the place is packed. The night I was there a group of knitters from South Dakota was holding a dinner meeting there. I noticed that they were all women except one large man in his forties. As we stood together in line waiting for a table, I complimented him on the unusual sweater he was wearing. He said, "Glad you like it. I knitted it myself to enter in a knitting contest." The sweater, green with white letters across the front, said, "Don't tell my mother that I knit. She thinks I play the piano in a whore house."

Fremont Dinner Train—Fremont

402-727-0615

F ew restaurants provide a view. Even fewer restaurants provide a moving view. You get both when you ride the Fremont Dinner Train. As you dine, the lush Elkhorn Valley glides gently by. Granted, this isn't the California Zephyr steaming through the Rocky Mountains, but the Elkhorn Valley does have a pastoral beauty that sets the perfect mood for combining a trip and dinner. Since you're not really going anywhere, except to Hooper and back, and you have no deadlines to meet, you can just sit back and relax, eat well, and relish the trip for the simple joy of doing something unique—nowhere else in the world is a dinner train pulled by a steam locomotive.

On the thirty mile round trip to Hooper you travel on track laid in 1869, later abandoned, and restored in 1986 by the Eastern Nebraska Chapter of the National Railway Historical Society. They also purchased and restored two wonderful vintage dining cars that are now pulled by a World War II steam engine.

The Fremont Dinner Train does an excellent job of recreating the elegant ambiance people used to expect from a railroad dining car. The interior of one car features bright red carpets and curtains, and oak woodwork. The second car, formerly of the Rock Island line, is a traditional style with original pictures and posters of rail travel on its walls. Both cars feature heavy, railroad-type china set on traditional white linen table cloths. The big band music of Tommy Dorsey, Glenn Miller, and Duke Ellington completes the vintage atmosphere.

The food includes a five-course meal on Fridays and Saturdays and a lighter three-course meal on Sundays. After a shaky start in its early years, the food has improved. The meals are good, although not outstanding. The menu varies by day and month. Depending on when you ride, entrees may include goose, salmon steak, prime rib, or quail. Vegetables and blueberry muffins are included.

If you're a railroad buff, you'll love the trip. If you're too young to have experienced the romance of the rails, you owe yourself a chance to savor travel in style, even if it's just to Hooper and back.

Mines Drug—Hooper

402-654-3527

What this country needs is a good five-cent cup of coffee. Well, Nebraska still has just what this country needs. If you are driving through Hooper and need some "break fluid," treat yourself to this rarity of the modern world at Mines Drug located on the historic main street of Hooper. You'll find an assortment of drugstore items, plus a coffee pot on the counter and a sign saying you can help yourself for the grand price of five cents.

Duane Mines has been holding the line on coffee prices for thirty-two years. Even in 1977, when coffee prices peaked at $107 per case, the price remained a nickel. Mine says he provides cheap coffee to keep the store busy. "It would be awfully quiet without the nickel coffee, and I don't like a quiet store." His idea works. Many Hooper regulars stop in two or three times a day. Mines says that out-of-towners who have heard of his price also stop in to sample a cup; sometimes they take a picture to prove that there really is a place in Nebraska still willing to supply a good five-cent cup of coffee.

The Office Bar and Grill—Hooper

402-654-3373

The Office Bar and Grill resides in the best-preserved restaurant building on the best-preserved main street in Nebraska. The west side of Hooper's main drag is just the way it was one hundred years ago. The street is lined with nine brick buildings in the American Renaissance style of architecture. (For you architectural buffs, there are also elements of Romanesque Revival and Italianate styles.) The buildings have survived because the town council, after a devastating fire in the 1880s, required that all new buildings be built of brick. Hooperites, recognizing the treasure in their midst, have refused to alter these buildings. The whole west side of main street is now included in the National Register of Historic Places. Adding charm to the buildings is a continuous tin awning that covers the sidewalk on the north end of the row. The original wooden benches lining the sidewalk have been worn slick by generations of overall-covered backsides.

One of the most interesting buildings is the one that houses the Office. Once inside, you realize that everything about these stately old buildings has been preserved: the original wood floors and pressed-tin ceiling remain, the walls are decorated with antiques, including the old Hooper High clock and a collection of Hooper High pennants.

The food is better than bar fare. I was there for lunch and the Office was packed. My hot roast beef sandwich was excellent, and I'll long remember the coconut cream pie topped with a full four inches of meringue.

Those who have taken the Pathfinder Train from Fremont to Hooper have undoubtedly discovered the Office. It's a gem, not only because of its historic significance, but because it is simply a comfortable, friendly place to have a beer or enjoy some good food.

Elsie's Cafe—Ithaca

402-623-4225

I I drove into Ithaca one noon hour looking for what had been touted as "great home-cooking-type road food." But when I got there the grain elevator was closed, the grocery store was closed, even the post office had a sign saying, "back at 1 p.m." Only one building showed any sign of life. Spotting lots of pickups parked out front and a faded sign saying Elsie's Cafe, I knew where to find everyone in town.

Recalling the calendar theory of restaurant selection (lots of calendars equals good chow) I peeked in the window. Only one calendar, but there was a great mug collection (which can substitute in a pinch). One whiff of the country cafe aroma, and I forgot all about tests for finding good food. The place was packed, too, with farmers, hunters, bikers, workers from the UNL field laboratories near Mead, and National Guardsmen attending the nearby training camp. All these folks couldn't be wrong.

I had heard that Elsie Williams, a self-described scratch cook, served home cooking in the same league with the very best. After I had polished off a plate of her pan-fried chicken, potato salad, green beans, and homemade bread, I decided that Elsie was almost as good a cook as my mom. And believe me, that's cookin'!

Then I asked Elsie about dessert. In fact, I asked her the key question when it comes to pie crust, "Do you make it with lard?" Granted this is not a question you want your cardiologist to know you're asking, but it's a guarantee of elite pie performance. Elsie answered that she rendered her own lard! The cherry pie did not disappoint; the flaky crust was as good as it gets. Elsie's Cafe passed all of the good eating tests.

Wagon Wheel—Laurel

402-256-3812

A well-stocked salad bar is a great place to practice gluttony by stealth. Everyone knows salad is good for you and not fattening—it's packed with vitamins and minerals and lacks cholesterol. That's what people think, and that's why they can eat great volumes of food at a salad bar and never be accused of being gluttons.

Sure, the Wagon Wheel is among Nebraska's best steak houses, but the heart of the place is its salad bar. The salad bar is so extensive that some diners have to sit and rest their legs half way through. Others could use a pack mule to carry their load. (I restrain myself, remembering the philosophy of one of my eating idols, Miss Piggy: "Never take more to eat than you can lift.")

In other parts of the country "salad bar" means a bowl of iceberg and a few carrots, radishes, and crackers. Not in Nebraska, and certainly not at the Wagon Wheel. The Wagon Wheel offers green salad, but why bother with lettuce when you can select from thirty to forty exotic dishes; it's more like a smorgasbord.

The selection includes sauerkraut salad, potato salad, pea salad, carrot salad, egg salad, cucumber and tomato salad, three-bean salad, and assorted fruit salads. There are also pasta salads, relishes, and pickled beets. Then there are dessert salads: jello, puddings, more fruits, cheeses, and ambrosia, a mixture of marshmallows, pineapple, mandarin oranges, and coconut.

These places always present a challenge: Do you throw caution to the wind and overeat at the salad bar like I did and then wish you'd ordered the chicken breast sandwich instead of the T-bone? Or do you exercise some degree of restraint at the salad bar—only one five pound refill—so that you don't feel guilty about the size of your steak? My advice, go with your gut feeling. But don't think for one moment that surreptitious refills at the Wagon Wheel salad bar are going to fool anyone.

Lyons Bakery and Cafe—Lyons

"These joints have names like Ethel's, Slick's, Bob's Pit Stop, and the Wild Horse Bar-B-Que. They use plastic tableware, serve spongy white bread, and are a far-sight less than elegant." That's how Oklahoma food writer, Michael Wallis describes the abundant barbecue restaurants of Oklahoma. Although Nebraskans have been able to handle Oklahoma in football lately, when it comes to barbecue, that mystical blend of fire, smoke, meat, and sauce; yes, barbecue that takes only twenty minutes and eight napkins to devour, Nebraska comes up short. In Nebraska the question is not how many good "Q" places there are, but rather are there any places that meet the high standards established in the South?

Superb barbecue requires a patient pitmaster with lots of time, access to hickory wood, some secret sauce, and quality beef. Nebraska had only the quality beef—until Pete Jones, a Texan with an optimistic attitude and a good recipe, moved to Lyons and turned the Lyons Cafe and Bakery into the barbecue oasis of northeastern Nebraska.

Jones, the only black man in this city of twelve

hundred, has won the hearts and stomachs of all and the affectionate moniker, "Uncle Pete." One of nineteen children, Pete comes from a long line of barbecue chefs. In fact, he says he can't remember when he couldn't cook. His grandfather started the Jones family barbecue tradition over 100 years ago by concocting the family's secret sauce recipe that Pete guards, like all barbecue pitmasters, with his life. Pete has been perfecting the sauce for the last twenty-five years. At a family reunion in 1983 his father encouraged him: "It's gettin' there," he remembers. His sauce is so secret that although his staff puts in the main ingredients, only Pete can add the special thirteenth ingredient when no one else is around.

After tasting the sauce, we can't blame him for wanting to keep it secret; it's right up there with the best. Spicy with a little heat, it has a gentle sweetness with just a hint of vinegar for tang. Brownish-red, it has sufficient thickness to prove it's been bred to cling, not drip. Most important, it enhances the flavor of the meat without overpowering it.

Pete also knows how to masterfully blend the smoke flavor into the meat. The cafe had a large oven in a back room which he has converted into his pit. He cooks the meat slowly so that the light smoke taste penetrates deeply into the meat, capturing it and converting it overnight into a barbecue masterpiece, a masterpiece that makes his patrons' taste buds tingle with delight and for which barbecue fanatics, even those from Oklahoma, would gladly sacrifice at least eight paper napkins per sitting. To put it another way, Pete's creation is the same kind of barbecue that experts Greg Johnson and Vince Staten describe in the July 1989 issue of *Food and Wine* as: "so meltingly tender and suffused with flavor that mere mortals ought to thank their lucky Wet Naps that the Gods didn't keep it to theirselves." Now you can understand why I've been back three times to sample Pete's specialty, lean Nebraska brisket, as well as his delicious beef and pork ribs.

The cafe is located in the middle of main street in Lyons. Its interior is plain, but bright and spotless, a definite improvement over most dumps in the South whose barbecue is so good the patrons are blinded to the surroundings. The rumor is that the cafe's name will soon be changed to Uncle Pete's, a name more appropriate for the treasures that lie within. Regardless of its name, though, this eatery can rightfully take its place alongside the Ethel's, Slick's, and Bob's of the barbecue world.

Note: Bad news! The Lyons Bakery and Cafe has passed away. I haven't been able to find out why it closed. It wasn't because of the quality of the food. Nebraska still needs a great barbecue place like this one.

The Bakery Cafe—Lynch

402-569-2646

O ver the years, Sally Wilson, owner of the Bakery Cafe in Lynch, has developed the psychic skills necessary to successfully run a small-town cafe. She can accurately predict what the locals are going to order as soon as they walk in the door. She exemplifies the attitude that small-town cafes strive to give extra service to their patrons.

Other unusual demands have required Sally's special attention. Sally recalls a man who brought his own can of pop into the Cafe and asked for a glass of ice. Another fellow came in to buy cinnamon for some cinnamon rolls he was making. To enable the men and women of Lynch to discuss and solve the problems of the world she also provided a large round table with full coffee service.

You may wonder how Sally has time to cook. But not to worry. Sally can cook. She serves a daily meat special, and cooks and bakes everything from scratch, including dinner rolls, sweet rolls, pies, and cookies.

However, her Sunday fried chicken has made her famous. I arrived at 11:40 a.m. one Sunday and by five after 12 the church crowd had packed the place. I ordered the chicken and wasn't disappointed. It tastes like she fixes it the same way as my grandmother used to from the buttermilk wash to a light dusting of flour, then gently into hot shortening in a black iron skillet.

Like my grandmother, Sally has an internal timer, one that magically tells her when to drop in the chicken and when to pluck it out. Sally's chicken turns out crisp, but not crusty. The teeth don't crunch into it— they glide past the auburn covering into the moist and tender meat below.

I topped off the dinner with flaky-crusted rhubarb pie, again the kind my grandmother used to make. When the fowl feast was over, and I was full to the brim, I knew I'd be back again. If I'd been a local, it would have been the next Sunday.

Sportsman's Bar and Grill—Meadow Grove

402-634-9293

"I n the act of the grillman molding a burger to plump perfection we see the modern world's equivalent of the medieval artisan. As he slaps and shapes the chopped meat, our host is transferring not only body heat to the burgers but also a little love." (Ralph Gardner, Jr., *Roadside Food*.)

Come to the Sportsman's Bar and Grill to watch your burger come alive. The open grill allows a complete view of the process. Unlike fast-food outlets where the process is hidden behind a wall and the product served in styrofoam, the Sportsman's bar and grill makes eating a spectator sport.

The feature at this eatery is the Grif-burger, a half-pound double cheeseburger that will destroy any factory-made burger in head-to-head competition. The locals claim it's the state's best burger. That's quite a boast in a state loaded with quality burgers, but I would agree that it's right up there with the best of them.

Stop in at the Sportman's and watch in anticipation as they produce for you, the great Grif-burger.

The Uptown Eating Establishment—Norfolk

326 Norfolk Avenue, 402-371-7171

You expect a lot from a restaurant that boldly proclaims: "A Dining Experience called . . . ONE OF A KIND." But the Uptown Eating Establishment in Norfolk lives up to its motto. The atmosphere is unique, and the quality and variety of the food is outstanding. In fact, the Uptown is the only restaurant in the state outside of the Lincoln-Omaha area that has received a three-diamond rating by the Automobile Association of America.

The Uptown is located in Norfolk in the historic old Kensington-Norfolk Hotel. The five story landmark has been recently renovated and includes the original grand ballroom and the hotel dining area that is now occupied by the Uptown.

The decor of the restaurant is classy 1940s art deco. The main dining room looks like a room out of a Bogart flick— black booths, southwestern pastels of peach and bronze, large planters, lazy ceiling fans straight out of *Casablanca*, and large glass lights.

The Uptown not only has atmosphere; it has history. Johnny Carson, a Norfolk native, did has first radio show in the dining room.

But by far the most unique thing about the Uptown is its innovative food. Just a glance at the menu tells you that the Uptown dares to be different. The meal will tell you that they succeed in a glorious manner. Where else in Nebraska can you find the following appetizers: salmon mousse, cool and creamy with a hint of dill; herring a la russe, herring marinated in cream wine sauce; golden caviar, fresh white-fish cavair with whipped cream cheese; beef terrine, elegant and silky pate of prime beef with rye toast. And that's just for starters.

The entrees are just as exotic. Here's a sample of the incredible variety: steak Johannesburg, tenderloin filet sauteed in butter with crab, shrimp, and other seafoods, topped with madiera cream sauce; salmon steak with crabmeat creole sauce; trout, locally grown; Swordfish, not locally grown, but cooked to perfection with fumet of lobster cream. It goes on and on. Special selections by the chef are featured (venison, pheasant, beef Wellington).

The Uptown is the winner of six international food awards, including the Gourmet Diner's Silver Spoon Award, and dozens of area awards. After trying the food. I heartily agree that the Uptown's chefs are creative. The Uptown uses only the finest whole, natural ingredients. They avoid all of no-no's of cooking—canned, pre-cooked, or processed items; convenience or gimmick; white sugar, grease, and refined salt. Instead, they stress natural ingredients such as honey and maple syrup, nut and seed oils, authentic Japanese tamari, a variety of beans, seeds, grains, and spices. They are even attentive to minute detail such as the ratio of sodium to potassium. The Uptown Eating Establishment fulfills its motto in every category—it is truly "One of A Kind!"

Corner Coffee Shop—Oakland

230 North Oakland, 402-685-5223

No need to go all the way to Sweden for Swedish rye bread. Just stop in Oakland, the self-proclaimed Swedish capital of Nebraska, and pick up a loaf or two at the Corner Coffee Shop.

The town of Oakland is over 125 years old, and the residents say that the Corner Coffee Shop has been there for most of those years. Located in a late nineteenth-century building only a half block from the railroad, the Cafe became popular with passengers as a place to refuel while waiting for the train to do the same. In the heyday of train travel, it was open twenty-four hours a day, seven days a week.

It's still popular today as a downtown gathering place; it was crowded at 11:00 a.m. when I was there the last time. The old wooden floor was worn smooth from years of use. The counter was full of farmers and townfolk, perched on the wooden stools with their feet resting on the iron rail below. The conversation was active, but the serious eaters at the counter were folded over their plates, elbows akimbo, oblivious to the banter.

I found the food hearty and deserving of its good reputation, but the real reason to stop at the coffee shop is the famous rye bread. It's light brown and soft, without the caraway seed that is so often characteristic of rye bread. It's sweet and makes delicious toast with homemade preserves slathered on top. They don't promote rye bread sales by the loaf; in fact, you have to talk them into it. So to avoid the disappointment of finding that they have sold out, always call ahead.

Stop off at the Corner Coffee Shop. Everyone does. In fact, the only bank robber in Oakland history stopped there shortly before he robbed the bank. He must have been craving the Swedish rye bread, found it sold-out, and then moved on to the second best asset in town.

Ye Ole Mill—Osceola

441 Hawkeye, 402-747-6441

The Polk County Courthouse guards the highest hill in Osceola like a medieval fortress. Tucked in among the stores that encircle the fortress is one my favorite slices of blue-plate America—Ye Ole Mill Cafe.

One of the things I enjoy most about classic small-town cafes is the banter between the staff and the regulars. The first time I visited the Mill, a waitress named Gladys (why are most waitresses in small-town cafes named Gladys or Dorothy or Agnes or Millie?) addressed a fellow in a cowboy hat and boots, "Floyd," she said, "I guess you're not a cowboy after all." Floyd was speechless. She continued, "Don't you know real cowboys never sit with their backs to the door." Floyd frowned, looked down, and then responded, "Gladys, have you read the thought for the day on this paper placemat? It's about you." Then he read, "Says here that a sharp tongue and a dull mind are found in the same head." Knowing she'd lost the first round, Gladys laughed, punched him on the shoulder, and responded, "Oh you. I'll get you yet."

During a typical lunch hour, the Mill is packed with a mix of local businessmen, farmers, ranchers, and travelers. You occasionally have to wait to be seated, a sure test of a great local cafe. The food is worth the wait. The consistently good home cooking is served in portions like your doting grandmother used to serve. To supplement your order, you can load up at a twenty-item salad bar which runs the gamut from sauerkraut to marshmallow fluff. A typical luncheon special of tuna casserole and salad bar is only $3.80.

I've been to the Mill several times and it's always a pleasure from the first sip of steaming soup to the last crumb of apple pie. I'm usually so full when I get to the cash register, I can't even muster the appetite to buy one of the gooey cinnamon rolls teasingly displayed in the front case.

If you're anywhere near Osceola in the evening, plan on hitting one of their buffet specials: Wednesday's-pizza, Thursday's-chicken, Friday's-fish, Saturday's-prime rib.

The Mill, unlike the court house, doesn't look like a fortress, but a meal there will leave you well fortified.

Fairview Cafe —Wahoo

1201 North Chestnut, 402-443-9941

I like to go to the Fairview about mid-morning. I can sit at the counter, study the daily grain prices on the blackboard in front of me, sip coffee, and enjoy a jumbo cinnamon roll while trading stories with the overall-clad farmers sitting on both sides of me. Because the Fairview is in a town rather than a village, its clientele is a mix of farmers, shopkeepers, travelers, workers, housewives, and kids.

Baking is the cafe's strong point. On the wall a plaque from the Wheat Division of the Nebraska Department of Agriculture honors its bread and rolls. The rolls are soft and fluffy, and the pies—particularly the raisin cream pie with a six-inch-high meringue—are claimed by some to be the best in the western world.

Several years ago I took a pee wee basketball team to a tournament near Wahoo. After the tournament we all went to the Fairview. The team's center, a redhead with an enormous appetite, affectionately known as Tubby, announced that he could eat more pie than anyone on the team. Willy, a skinny guard, bet a bag of bubble gum that Tubby couldn't eat a whole pie. Tubby readily accepted the bet and proceeded to eat one, three, five pieces of the raisin cream pie. With three pieces left, Tubby began to slow. Pie eaters, like marathoners, sometimes hit a wall, and their pace slows. As Tubby barely finished his seventh piece, Willy thought the bet was secure. Tubby looked beaten. Not wanting him to get sick on the drive home, I cautioned, "If you eat one more piece of pie, you're going to ex-lode." Tubby paused, looked up from the pie, glanced at his teammates, and said, "Pass the pie . . . and stand back!"

In *Wig Wag* magazine Scott Sander describes the

kind of food served at the Fairview. "I see my grandmother, barefoot and bulky, mixing dough with her fingers. Then I realize that everything . . . [it] serves she would have served. This is farm food, loaded with enough sugar and fat to power a body through a slogging day of work, food you could fix out of your own garden and chicken coop and pigpen, food prepared without sauces or spices, cooked the quickest way, as women with chores to do and a passel of mouths to feed would cook it."

Yes, this is farm food. It's hot roast beef with gravy-smothered mashed potatoes, ham dinners, casseroles, hearty soups, and burgers. My favorites are the chicken soup with thick homemade noodles, chicken and biscuits, and corned beef. The calorie-conscious would starve here.

After a big lunch at the Fairview, Wahoo's farmers are able to work in the field all afternoon. I probably could myself, after a two-hour nap.

OK Market—Wahoo

532 North Linden, 402-443-3015

Wahoo is the hometown of movie producer Darryl Zanuck, baseballer Sam Crawford, composer Howard Hanson, Nobel Prize winner Dr. George Beatle, and the nationally famous Wahoo Weiner. While these great men are now long gone, the weiner, born in 1919, lives on at the OK Market.

The Market offers far more than the original weiner. You can also buy garlic shorties, polish sausage, cream sausage, and potato sausage. In fact, they have twenty-three different sausage recipes that they prepare periodically. Of course, the weiners or sausages are not shrink-wrapped or encased in plastic; they are linked together the old-fashioned way in natural casings just like back in the 20s.

Not satisfied with having the best weiners and sausage in Nebraska, owner Hal Horak has installed a new deli where he says they've "gone beyond home cooking to farm-style cooking." It's not only good and served in generous portions but a daily special, ranging from fried chicken, pork steak, or sauerkraut and dumplings, still costs no more than $2.50.

In addition to reviving the weiner tradition, Horak has completely restored the Market since taking over in 1989. He used a picture from the 1920s as his guide in faithfully reproducing the two-tone brown interior. And on the outside he retained the classic, oval-shaped, green "Meat" sign, faded just as he found it. The building has been proposed for the National Register of Historic Places.

The noon I was there, the little place was packed. I had to wait for a table, but it was worth it. I started with an enormous bowl of black bean and sausage soup, and next moved to the Wahoo Weiners, coarsely ground beef with a slight peppery taste served on a soft bun and topped with fried onions.

There are some good hot dogs in this state, but Wahoo Weiners fall into an elite category usually reserved for culinary treasures. This soup-and-dog lunch more than satisfied; it also whetted my appetite for more. On the way out, I purchased weiners-to-go at the meat counter: some finely ground, some coarsely ground, some garlic-seasoned, and some chubby polish sausages. Just a sample, you see.

Significant Others—Northeast

Cafe on Main —Blair
402-426-2311

The owners of the Cafe have transformed an old building in downtown Blair into a trendy, post-modern cafe common in L.A., but totally unexpected in Blair.

The original tin ceiling and brick walls have been retained and combined with sculpture and bright colors—whites, purples, and turquoise—for an exciting, eclectic look.

This lunch-only cafe offers a sophisticated and imaginative menu. Some of the daily specials are New Wave Burgers, herbed rainbow trout, four-cheese sandwich, couscous chicken, and chicken and shrimp florentine. There are fresh fish selections, Italian and Mexican dishes, sandwiches, and salad specialties (cobb, terriyaki, chicken, seafood, and spinach).

Incidently, as you drive into town from the south, if you're so hungry you can't wait to get to the Cafe on Main, there's a shop that sells bait, and carp dinners. Make sure they get your order straight.

Muffin Shoppe—Columbus
2905 14th St.
402-563-333

Ladies-who-lunch flock here for quiche, salads, and expansive desserts. Fresh muffins daily, of course. In a restored home with a neighboring house attached as an upscale gift shop.

Euni's Place—Dixon
402-584-9309

The place to go in Dixon is a small metal building rebuilt by the village after the last Place burned. Euni is a jolly woman who serves up pizza with big flavor, good burgers, and cheap, delicious daily specials. Casual, family atmosphere— Euni's two-year-old granddaughter crawled around on the bar as I sipped a soda.

The Longbranch—Leshara
402-721-8882

I whooped it up one night with friends at the Longbranch. I'm not sure whether it was the fine company, the beverages, or the Longbranch itself that made it a great evening. But if on a Saturday night you want to pull on clean jeans, eat a great slab of prime rib, and do a little dancing to a one-woman band, check out the Longbranch. Ignore the "For Sale" sign; it's been there forever. Based on the crowd that night, the owner probably can't afford to sell for less than the price of the Brooklyn Bridge.

Beef 'n Stuff—Page
402-338-5348

Converted machine shed serves low-grease meals, prohibits smoking, and offers beef with no additives. Just walk in and you'll feel healthier, but watch out for the high-calorie country-comfort food.

Headquarters —Plainview
402-582-4710

Typical cafe grub served at unique harvest-crew-sized tables. The arrangement throws strangers in with locals who look you over first like the newest gunfighter in town, but treat you like family once the food comes and the conversation starts again. The owner periodically publishes humorous ads in the local newspaper about his wife's family and those few friends good-natured enough to put up with his ribbing.

Hotel Wakefield—Wakefield
402-287-9026

Relic hotel with remodeled rooms. Spend a getaway weekend in exotic Wakefield. Beef and gourmet dishes, including quiche and omelettes. Sunday champagne brunch is a highlight.

Neligh House—West Point
402-372-3400

Family restaurant with lavish marble staircase and a wooden banister from old St. Joseph's Hospital in Omaha. Good stick-to-your-ribs cooking. Earlier Neligh House specialized in strawberry shortcake; that tradition lives on.

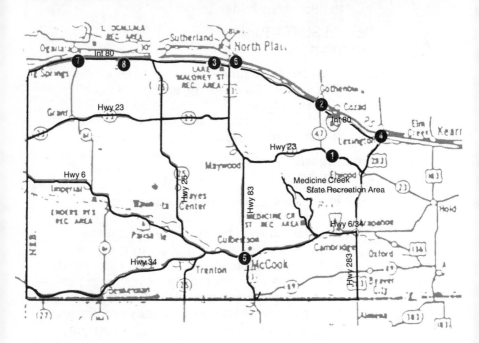

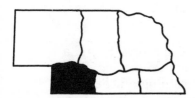

Southwest

1. Eustis—The Pool Hall
2. Gothenburg—Bonnie's Swede Cafe
3. Hershey—Butch's Bar
4. Lexington—Little Paris
5. McCook—Atch's Coppermill
6. North Platte—Skelly Inn
   Sugar Spoon
7. Ogallala—Cassel's Family Restaurant
8. Paxton—Ole's Big Game Bar

Nebraska Obscurata

Travel writers Alan Boye and D. Ray Wilson have outlined countless facts about the Cornhusker state. I've found, however, that the more interesting Nebraska facts are the obscure ones. I've dug deep into Nebraska lore to discover as yet unheard-of obscurities. Here are some of the most riveting examples:

■ Early settlers of Brock, a village in southeastern Nebraska, had a heck of a time deciding on a town name. They tried Dayton, and then a series of six others before finally choosing plain old Brock. One of the top contenders was Podunk. Nothing original about Podunk; half the towns in the state have been called Podunk at one time or another. In fact, folks from the East Coast call the whole darn state Podunk.

■ Roger Welsch says Dannebrog is home of the Liars' Hall of Fame. I don't believe him.

■ Devil's Nest, a wild section of land overlooking the Missouri River and now Lewis and Clark Lake, was said to be a hideway of Jesse James and other rustlers and thieves. Investors who were heldup by the now defunct resort development of Devil's Nest think rustlers and thieves are still hiding there.

> The first courthouse in Arthur County was a covered wagon.

■ Arthur is the home of the only baled hay church in the world. Bales of hay were stacked and plastered over for a stucco-like appearance. On a slow Sunday, the preacher often wondered if there weren't more varmints in the walls than in the pews.

■ The first courthouse in Arthur County was a covered wagon. It was the country's only mobile courthouse. The next courthouse was a tent. They built a fence around it to keep the cattle out (a great idea for keeping the bull out of the legal system). After the tent blew away, Arthur residents brought a one-room homesteader's shack into town for the courthouse. It was the smallest courthouse in America until 1962. You could a get marriage license, file a deed, plead guilty, and get a divorce all in the same room, and all at the same time.

■ An early Plattsmouth clothing store kept monkeys in a tree in its front window. That's where the term "monkey suit" was invented.

■ In the spring of 1877, Plattsmouth recorded its only earthquake. Actually, it wasn't an earthquake; it was the clothing store proprietor discovering what escaped monkeys can do to the inside of a store.

Interfaith Church
Keystone

■ In 1908, a church was built in Keystone to serve two congregations, Catholic and Protestant. Special dispensation was given by the Pope to allow dual services in the building. With a Catholic altar at one end and a

Protestant altar at the other, pews were hinged to flip over and be of service to either faith. This is the first known example of a group-conversion experience.

■Kool-Aid was invented near Beaver City in the little town of Henley. My theory is that the water was so bad, towns-folk put everything they could think of into it to make it taste good enough to drink.

■In 1891, Monroe Barryman set the world hand cornhusking record in an Eagle, Nebraska, cornhusking contest. He picked 9100 pounds of corn in eleven hours. In 1986, Katherine's father, Louie Brauer, sixty-four, won the Nebraska State Hand Cornhusking Championship: 779 pounds in thirty minutes. Inspired by Louie's success, the following year I entered the contest and set a new record. Little did I know that the judges would penalize me and subtract pounds for each ear left on the stalk and for failing to thoroughly husk the ears I managed to pick. When my penalty pounds were subtracted from the pounds picked, my new records was . . . minus fifty-three pounds.

■Nebraska has been a hotbed of UFO sightings. Several have involved cattle. For example, in 1897 a cigar-shaped ship was observed hovering over a beef herd. A cable was lowered out of the ship and fat steer was hoisted into the spaceship and whisked away. Hence the phrase, "Where's the beef?"

■On the edge of Purdum, a Sandhills burg of about thirty people, there's a sign that reads "Purdum, Next Six Exits." Purdum, however, is so small that by the time you get there, you're past it.

■The town of Greeley still sports a sign that reads "Greeley, Home of 580 Friendly People and a Few Old Crabs." Years ago, I passed through Greeley with my then-eight-year-old son who wanted to stop at the local cafe after reading the sign. When we walked in, there

Greeley Town
Sign, Greeley

wasn't a smile in sight. An ill-tempered waitress
frowned as she asked: "Whaddya want?" In the back of
the dining room two farmers argued about the
weather. My son turned to me and said, "Dad, I think
we've found a nest of old crabs."

■ The largest hailstone in the U.S. fell near Potter
in 1928. It was seventeen inches around and weighed
nearly two pounds. Didn't last long though. Didn't
have a snowball's chance in . . . well, Potter is hotter.

308-486-3801

In 1910 Carrie Nation of the Women's Christian Temperance Union wrote the following to the owner of the Pool Hall in Eustis, "I will soon have finished my work in Kansas and then will turn my attention to the murder dens of Nebraska. Nothing can stop me. I have three hundred women enlisted in this work, and no matter what happens to me, the work will go on. Every saloon on the line you live on has been warned to close up or suffer the consequences. I will chop your infernal old whiskey shop into kindlin' wood and pour out your vile stuff into the street. I will be there on the 15th or 16th, and my work will be sure and lasting." Fortunately for the Pool Hall, Carrie Nation was arrested in Kansas before reaching Eustis. Ironically, she may have gotten excited over nothing: Johnny Frew, son of the founder of the Pool Hall, relates that beer wasn't even sold in the Hall until after Prohibition, and no distilled spirits were sold until early in the 1980s!

Not only has the Pool Hall survived, but Carrie Nation would probably be dismayed to know that it is now owned by a woman, Connie Koch. While growing up in Eustis, Connie used to go to the Pool Hall with her dad, and she learned how to play snooker and pool from Johnny Frew, the former owner from whom she bought the Pool Hall in 1976.

Connie kept the original Pool Hall's snooker table and a pool table that had been a part of the business since the 1960s. As you enter you walk past these tables to a large oak bar with a rich design and stained glass back. Brick walls are covered with pink flamingos (the bar logo), flowers, antiques, and mirrors. The wooden floors glow with the reflection of four antique lamps hung from the tin ceiling.

Although Eustis is a German community, the food at the Pool Hall is primarily Mexican. Connie wisely reasoned that Eustis's German citizens weren't going to come to the Pool Hall to get what they could get at home, and Mexican specialties have been a big success. She serves a wide variety of dishes including burritos, tacos, and rellenos (cheese and mild chili strips wrapped in an egg-batter shell topped with red or green chiles). In addition, the bar serves the usual burgers and steak, plus an outstanding polish sausage sandwich with kraut, German mustard, and horse-radish on the side, all described in a humorous newspaper-format menu. For example, a dish called "anti-vampire chile" got its name when Rose (probably the cook) mistook bulbs of garlic for cloves of garlic and permanently freed Frontier County of vampires. It's strictly authentic Mexican stuff with chunks of beef and pork in green chile sauce, served with rice, beans, and a tortilla.

For appetizers I enjoyed the nachos with homemade chips and one of the most creative foods I have found in my travels—Nebraska corn nuggets. Each marble-size deep fried morsel contained a kernel of creamed corn, crisp on the outside and moist on the inside. As the menu says, "It's a must for the corn-fed Nebraskan."

Times have changed since the WCTU threatened the Pool Hall. Carrie Nation might feel that the current Pool Hall's not such a bad place after all. In fact, if she happened to get one of Connie's hot chiles, she might welcome a cold beer to wash it down.

Little Paris—Lexington

201 East 5th St., 308-324-5887

The Little Paris in Lexington doesn't serve boeuf bourguignon, truffles, escargots, or mousse de chocolat. (It does, however, offer French toast.) The walls sport no travel posters of Notre Dame Cathedral or the Eiffel Tower. Why, then, the name? The Little Paris is owned by Tom and Deborah Paris. Ahhh, but of course.

I just stumbled onto this restaurant located in a red brick building, former home of the town's Chevy dealer. There was really nothing unusual about it, but the food was good the first time I tried it, and it has been good on return visits. It's a family kind of place, clean and neat. The food is well prepared and nicely presented. Its specials feature American comfort food, like pot roast and mashed potatoes or chicken-fried steak and green beans. For lunch it offers an abundant soup, salad, and sandwich bar. Everything is homemade and tastes that way.

The baked goods are the highlight of the Little Paris. I've tried several great cream pies, as well as the standard flaky-crusted fruit varieties, and I keep coming back for more. Road food experts have long recommended several well-known places straddling the interstate for great cinnamon and pecan rolls. I've tried 'em and forgotten about 'em, but I won't forget about Little Paris's rolls.

The folks are friendly at the Little Paris. But when leaving Paris, don't expect to hear "Merci" or "Bon soir." You'll just get the familiar Nebraska farewell, "Thanks, have a nice day."

Having a big dinner party this weekend and want to serve something memorable for dessert? You might want to phone the Sugar Spoon in North Platte. You'll soon have a special kind of cheesecake that's guaranteed to earn raves.

The Sugar Spoon is a Horatio Alger-type success story. Woman needs money, has a great recipe and can cook, starts making cheesecake in her kitchen, travels across the state peddling her product which soon sells so well she has to expand out of her kitchen to her own bakery, and before long she is shipping the product across the country. That's the success story of Lu Clinton and the Sugar Spoon.

I had my first taste of Sugar Spoon cheesecake when someone shipped some to me frozen in a styrofoam container. I'm ordinarily not a big cheesecake fan—too heavy, too rich, too many calories in trade for a taste that doesn't overwhelm me. But believe me, this cheesecake is different from the typical offering; it's more like a frozen cream pie, available in fifteen exotic flavors, including peaches and cream, double chocolate or strawberry Amaretto, Irish cream, and creme de menthe. You can even get a twelve-flavor sampler.

Sugar Spoon cheesecake is made from natural ingredients and contains no flour. It's frozen, not too sweet, and may be one of the best desserts in the universe.

The price for a cake, which weighs about three pounds and can serve twelve, ranges from $15 to $20. They make glorious gifts for friends who enjoy food and appreciate something really different. Whether you want to treat yourself, need a dessert for your next party, or want to surprise someone with a gourmet gift,

Sugar Spoon cheesecake fits the bill. To order toll-free call 1-800-228-0052

Cassel's Family Restaurant—Ogallala

308-284-2088

I f you're going to get stranded in one of Nebraska's blizzards, do it at a great place to eat. That's what many travelers did when the blizzard of '83 closed the interstate. They stopped at Cassel's and passed the time by eating as many great breakfast

dishes as they could. In between hearty meals of pancakes and scrambled eggs (supply trucks couldn't get through either so they had to limit the menu), guests slept in the booths using tablecloths for blankets. Is there no end to Nebraska hospitality?

Cassel's has been serving great food for over nineteen years. A family operation, it was founded by Paul L. Cassel and is now run by his son Tom and wife Dee. They have continued the tradition of good food, with an emphasis on pancakes. Their specialities include peanutty chocolate pancakes, german apple pancakes (browned popovers puffed and topped with spiced apples), and orange blossom crepes (thin strawberry pancakes drizzled with a delicate orange sauce).

So if you've been driving hard on the interstate and need a break, stop at Cassel's, even if it isn't snowing.

Ole's Big Game Lounge—Paxton

308-239-7500

Did you ever eat a buffalo burger with an eleven-foot, 1500-pound polar bear looking over your shoulder? Sit down in a booth after conveniently hanging your hat on a five foot spread of moose antlers? Have a drink in an establishment opened one minute after the repeal of prohibition in 1933? See a bar from the infamous Cheyenne Frontier Hotel taken in payment for pitching a ballgame? If the answer to any of these questions is no, you better pack the old station wagon and head down the Interstate to Ole's Big Game Lounge in Paxton.

World-famous hunter Ole Herstedt has assembled one of the largest private collections of big game trophies in the world—over two hundred in all. In addition to the polar bear, there is elephant, giraffe, buffalo, leopard, elk, jaguar, python, and, of course the rare Nebraska jackalope (a cross between a rabbit and an antelope). Ole's is really a big hunting lodge with trophies mounted on rustic, knotty-pine walls. Non-hunters may cringe, but the decor represents an era when conservation of animals was not a high priority.

When Ole retired in 1988 he sold the bar to two local men in their late twenties because he just couldn't stand to see it closed and his collection moved out of Paxton. The new owners, farmer Tim Holzfaster and elevator manager Brent Gries, who had no experience in the bar and restaurant business, spent a lot of time there as children with their families. They particularly remember playing pool on two tables in the back, supervised by Ole's mother.

Although the new owners vowed not to alter the trophy collection, they have made some rather dramatic changes in the operation. The only grub you used to be able to get at Ole's was a hot dog and a hard-boiled egg from a huge jar on the bar. Holzfaster and Gries have installed a sparkling stainless-steel kitchen so Ole's now serves a complete menu of good food at very reasonable prices. The steaks, cut fresh daily, are excellent, and reasonably priced, particularly with the inflation-free top price of $8.95. They also offer a buffalo burger, labeled the delicacy of the plains, for $2.50 and Rocky Mountain Oysters, advertised as so good you'll go nuts over them.

So when it's a jungle out there, head for Ole's.

Too Tough To Die

The small-town cafe is the most importance business in town. It's a gathering place, a place to laugh, to joke and to visit with friends. It's also where people stop in for a cup of coffee and to talk about the crops and the weather, to complain about politics, and discuss Friday's high school game. One woman in her eighties explained, "I don't know what I'd do if we didn't have a cafe. Where would I go to visit with my friends?" Then she smiled and added, "I guess we'd just have to start spending more time in the tavern."

But a cafe's function goes beyond social. It's the town's communication center—a place to learn about and spread the the news. A farmer in Spaulding told me, "The nearest town with a newspaper is miles away and it only comes out once a week. I go to our cafe to find out what the heck's going on around here." Without the cafe, friends would be slower to know that Millie Amen had a baby girl, that Olive Creek is running bank full, or that the volunteer fire department is having a pork feed next month.

> "I don't know what I'd do if we didn't have a cafe."

Yes, Nebraskans know the cafe is a place worth keeping, but just as important, they realize that the survival of the town cafe is not only the cafe owner's problem—it's the responsibility of the whole community.

Communities across the state are taking innovative steps to preserve their treasured cafes. Here are some of the bootstrapping techniques being used by Nebraskans to keep their cafes:

Euni's Place, Dixon: About three years ago a fire reduced Euni's Place to ashes, and left Dixon without a cafe. In a large town such a fire would be unfortunate, but rebuilding it would be the owner's burden, not the community's. Not so in Dixon. Within a few weeks, the community was figuring out how to rebuild Euni's Place. And rebuilt it was. Community fundraisers were held and a new fireproof metal building now houses Euni's Place, assuring the community that Euni Diedecker will continue to provide this town of 150 with the best homemade pizza for miles around.

Jewell Diner
Mullen

D and P Diner, Madrid: The first thing Peg Haden, owner of the D and P Diner, thought as she lay ill in a Denver hospital was, "What is going to happen to the meals I fix for my senior citizens?" Seniors had become accustomed to gathering for lunch every day at the D and P. In addition, Peg had transported senior meals to Elsie, eight miles away, on Mondays, Wednesdays, and Fridays. But operating the only cafe in this town of 280, it was not only the seniors that she worried about. Thoughts of selling or closing ran through her mind.

There was nothing to worry about. The community simply took over. Volunteers ran the D and P for the six weeks that Peg was in the hospital. Residents and customers sat down together and worked out volunteer schedules for all of the required duties. For example, Irma Jeffries, eighty-one, was assigned to dishwashing duties. Dorothy Vlasin, who once had been a co-owner with Peg, organized food preparation. Verla Terry, the only paid employee, made sure that the place got opened and closed. George Tjaden supplied fresh flowers and produce from his garden. After school, when the high school kids came in droves, one or two of them got behind the counter to keep things running smoothly.

> Residents and customers sat down together and worked out volunteer schedules for all of the required duties.

Peg is back now and is even more grateful that she lives in a small town. The D and P is a survivor—thanks to the citizens of the Madrid area.

Korner Kafe, Byron: In 1976 the last cafe in town closed. Realizing the importance of a cafe, the town organized the Byron Community Association for the purpose of finding a way to re-open a cafe in Byron. The association, first headed by dairy farmer Howard Reinke, bought an old bar and converted it into the Korner Kafe. The original cleanup and construction was a joint effort of the men and women in the community.

Not only does the Kafe feed the community in general, but it, like many other small-town cafes, is the source of a daily hot meal for the community's senior citizens. August Kniep, ninety-one, said he eats there everyday. "It's my one big meal a day. For the others, which I have to fix, it's strictly light and basic."

The ladies who run the Kafe also admit that they enjoy the social aspect. Marie Harms, in her late seventies, relates, "Coming here and being with others is a lot better than just sitting at home alone. It makes life more fun and gives me the satisfaction of knowing that I am helping others in the community."

Nettie's Kitchen, Gurley: Several years ago Nettie Drake's landlord told her that she'd have to move out of the building in which she operated Nettie's Kitchen. It didn't take long for Gurley-area residents to solve Nettie's problem. Twenty-four people simply bought the building and rented it to Nettie at a very reasonable rate. Recently Jolene Egging and her family took over the lease and the Kitchen became the Village-In. Jolene continues the good cooking tradition and serves an unusual pie which is a combination of coconut and pineapple, called, "Darn good pie!" I thought it was even better than that.

The Market, Oshkosh: When this cafe closed, the local banker, who owned the building, didn't give up. He hired a former cook to run it for a year. When she proved she could do it, he loaned her the money to buy it herself. Today it's thriving.

Butte Cafe, Butte: Another example of Nebraska ingenuity is the Butte Cafe. The only cafe in town, it is owned by the city of Butte. Citizens donated $27,000 and volunteers worked on the construction. The town leases the cafe for $125 a month to Andy Stevens, a twenty-eight-year-old who got his cooking experience in the army and in two cafes in South Dakota. Andy's mother, grateful to the town for bringing her son back home and the cafe back as well, recently told a *Lincoln Journal* reporter: "This (town) is Love, Nebraska; that's how I feel."

Significant Others —Southwest

Bonnie's Swede Cafe—Gothenburg
308-537-7446

Typical main street cafe with mainstreet home cooking. Tasty special, by golly: slab of meatloaf the size of a loaf of bread, 'taters, green beans, and coffee for $3.95. I supplemented the special with Swedish potato soup and strawberry pie. That Bonnie can cook, by Yiminy!

Butch's Bar—Hershey
100 First St.
308-368-7231

Flashing sign says, "Now serving breakfast," but beef is the star at Butch's. The prime rib special draws a crowd on Thursdays through Saturdays. Best mahi-mahi north of the Platte.

Atch's Coppermill—McCook
308-345-2296

Where else can you dine with a golf-course view and eat steak that lists at only 29 cents (note the small print, "With meat, $10.75"). Also, try the Coppermill filet bearnaise. Like other Atch's in the state, the menu is varied and the food good.

Skelly Inn—North Platte
308-532-88720

Next door to a Texaco station in North Platte is a small red-brick building—the Skelly Inn. The sign out front says, "Home Cook'n so-o-o good you'd think Mom was in the kitchen."

After a huge skillet of eggs, bacon, hash browns and toast (grand total $3.65) and topping it off with one of their famous cinnamon rolls, I went back to the kitchen to look for Mom.

SOUTH CENTRAL REGION

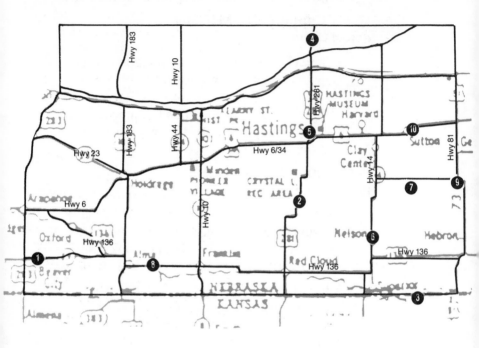

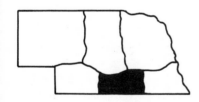

South Central

1. Beaver City—The Ole Panhandler
2. Blue Hill—Goody's Place
3. Byron—Korner Kafe
4. Grand Island—Coney Island Lunch Room
   Conoco Cafe
   Dreisbach's
   G.I. Candy Kitchen and Cafe
   Nonna's Palazzo
5. Hastings—Front Porch
   LoRayne's
6. Nelson—Sportsmen's Corner Steakhouse
7. Ong—Country Village Cafe
8. Republican City—Little Mexico
9. Strang—Strang Tavern
10. Sutton—The Big Idea

RoadArt

"There's something odd about Nebraska. If you ask anyone who has spent a day driving across the state, border to border, Nebraska seems to be nothing but open space. Willa Cather expressed it best in *My Antonia* when one of her main characters, newly arrived from Virginia, stepped off the train and said, "There was nothing but land: not a country at all, but the material out of which countries are made . . . ."

I noticed this vast emptiness when I moved here twenty-seven years ago. My native state has more trees, more hills, more cities, more people, much less open space and sky. In Nebraska, it seems as if there was no "there" there—only empty spaces. All this space can cause some folks to feel a little uneasy. In fact, this feeling often becomes more than just uneasiness—it becomes a fear. I call this fear, "Nondecoagoraphobia," the fear of undecorated spaces.

> . . . there are few spots in this state where some earnest citizen hasn't done his or her best to fill the empty space with some small bit of artistic memorabilia.

Many who experience this fear simply flee the state. Those who stay attempt to cope by decorating. As a result, there are few spots in this state where some earnest citizen hasn't done his or her best to fill the empty space with some small bit of artistic memorabilia. These objets d'art—attempts to remedy the fear of undecorated spaces—are what I call RoadArt.

In rural Nebraska, RoadArt comes in many forms. For example, farmers favor mailbox art. Drive the gravel farm roads. You'll see welded horseshoe mailboxes, cream separator mailboxes, plow mailboxes, and, of course, one of Nebraska's most prominent forms of mailbox humor, the box posted ten feet high labeled Air Mail. Ranchers favor hanging their old boots on fence posts. Good examples of this can be found near Wauneta and Lynch where the boot posts stretch for miles. The effect is puzzling, but the boots do fill space and bring a touch of civilization to an otherwise un-spoiled landscape.

Towns have different space-filling tricks. Check out the town squares or parks. These spaces can be in-explicably filled with armaments—airplanes, artillery pieces, tanks, and cannonballs. Kimball decorates its park with modern hardware, a hundred-foot-long Titan

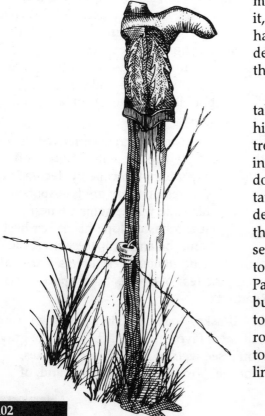

missile. Come to think of it, there's enough military hardware around to defend the whole state in the event of enemy attack.

Some towns are taking RoadArt to a higher level. The new trend is the artistic paint-ing of city water towers. I don't mean the spon-taneous form often demonstrated by en-thusiastic high school seniors; I'm referring to town-sanctioned painting. Papillion sports a monarch butterfly on its water tower, O'Neill a sham-rock, Gretna a dragon, Sut-ton a mustang, and Ueh-ling a panther. The best example of this elevated RoadArt is the water tower in Ogallala, painted to resemble a flying saucer encircled with flashing lights. Mayor Paul Cassel calls it "America's first flying saucer decoy." It illustrates a new use for RoadArt: attracting tourists (if they're from outer space).

RoadArt in the residential areas of Nebraska towns is expressed in the form of yard ornaments—whirl-a-gigs, twirling sunflowers, colorful windsocks, spinning propellers, and shiny globes simply sitting on pedestals. No practical function have they; yard ornaments just decorate space.

Within a few miles of where you live, wherever you live in Nebraska, you'll find examples of RoadArt. Near where we live west of Lincoln, there's a twenty-foot Loch Ness monster in the front yard of an acreage. A creative soul has cut different-sized tractor tires in half and placed them on the ground in a way that, if the ground were water, it would look like part of the serpent's body is in the water and part of it is out. Southwest of here is a large log in front of a house, painted black with fins and a conning tower. The words, "*USS Stelling*," are painted on this prairie dry-docked submarine.

At the Milford Exit on the I-80, a herd of flat, wooden buffalo cutouts perpetually graze in the pasture near large metal teepees (and just across the road from the world's largest prairie schooner).

Just outside of Chadron, Ken Hollrah, a transplanted Arizonan and chronic nondecoagoraphobic, has decorated the front of his Park View Store, next to the entrance to Chadron State Park, with a twenty-two-foot tall cactus carved from the trunk of a dead elm tree. The *Omaha World-Herald* quotes Hollrah,

"I just missed those big, old cactuses they have down in the desert, and, well, there was this big old dead tree standing just outside the door. So I figured why not make myself feel at home." The depth of Hollrah's malady is further demonstrated by his inability to stop embellishing his RoadArt. "I may have set a record for using the most toothpicks in a three-month span," he claims. "I've already used 38,000 toothpicks that I walnut-stained for stickers on the cactus. It'll have close to 50,000 when I get it all done."

In 1975, as part of a bicentennial project, Nebraska decided to decorate five hundred miles of I-80 with a sculpture garden. This created great controversy because there were those who recognized the abundance of accomplished RoadArtists in this state and believed that Nebraskans should create the sculpture garden themselves. (One of the most outspoken advocates of this approach was a welder from near Litchfield who had filled his yard with welded iron replicas of windmills, spaceships, and cowboys.) All ten of the pieces selected, however, were created by out-of-state artists. One such artist, John Raimondi, fanned the flames of artistic controversy by creating "Erma's Desire," an assemblage of rusted, pointed beams, thrusting up from the earth. Some people, by a great stretch of the imagination, interpreted this sculture as erotic. Whatever the interpretation, the I-80 sculpture project, billed as the world's largest sculpture garden, certainly fulfills our need to fill.

> Nebraska's most recent example of major RoadArt is Carhenge

Nebraska's most recent example of major RoadArt is Carhenge. This roadside attraction has created enough commotion to deserve national attention. I had never heard of Carhenge before I saw it one winter day as I was driving north a few miles out of Alliance. Looking out across a field, I was stunned to see a circle of twenty-two half-buried cars. The cars, mostly Plymouths, Fords, and Chevrolets with a Cadillac and an ambulance thrown in, were painted a battleship gray and arranged in a replica of England's prehistoric Stonehenge. Perhaps it was the grayness of the day and the grayness of the cars, but I found the image stark and exciting. Others agree. The reaction of Patrick Hund, a visitor from Alaska, was recorded in the *Lincoln Journal*; "It sent chills up my spine." he said. Others call it an eyesore. At an Alliance city council meeting, one resident went so far as to equate it with a house of ill-repute for the base way it stimulates economic activity.

In the northeastern part of the state is an example of a different form of Roadart, or shall I say RockArt. Favored in this area are numerous yard decorations

Carhenge
Alliance

made of round field stones. The finest example is located two blocks north of the main street of Lyons. The house is surrounded by stone-age relics, literally. You'll find a shed made of field stones, a wishing well, a small bridge, planters, terraces, walls, and, for all I know, a kennel and a compost pile of field stones. The creator seemed to have a yearning for concrete and rock and plenty of time on his or her hands. The result is creation for its own sake—no grand intent, no plan, no real reason to speak of. It is a monument to what one Nebraskan will do with time and undecorated surfaces.

> If one small stone sculpture looks good, twenty will be breath-taking.

When nondecoagoraphobia reaches the advanced stage, it seems to wipe out all creative urges in the victim. He or she can only resort to repetitive RoadArt. If one small stone sculpture looks good, twenty will be breath-taking. First a small deer springs up in the flower beds, next it's a deer family, then a whole herd. Or it can manifest itself in multiple wooden sillouettes of squat, elderly women bending over their gardens, wooden bloomers in full view. The most serious case I've observed was a yard where first there was only one elderly woman gardener, but the next time I drove by there was a wooden gentleman in overalls standing next to her, his hand on her rump. (This loving couple can be viewed regularly across the street to the east as you exit the Saline County Courthouse in Wilber.)

I'm proud to say that I've successfully resisted the urge to decorate my property with useless RoadArt. No decorative deer or cutouts of ladies' backsides in my yard. Everything there is strictly functional. My orange-and-red roadrunner whirl-a-gig mounted near my garden keeps the birds from eating my strawberries. My miniature red and white windmill with Herbie Husker mounted on top is placed outside the living room window only so I can determine wind direction. The seven giant red, orange, and blue plastic butterflies, whose wings flutter in the breeze, are mounted on the sliding-glass patio doors only to keep guests from inadvertently walking into them. And, of course, everyone needs a rain gauge; mine just happens to be held upright in the beak of a flamingo.

Goody's Place—Blue Hill

522 West Gage, 402-756-3351

G oody's Place in Blue Hill keeps its prices down by keeping a tight rein on expenses. Perhaps that's why they don't even have a sign on the outside of the cafe. Advertising is an expense that Goody's doesn't need. They figure if you're around Blue Hill for long you'll hear about it anyway.

This philosophy works fine unless you're from out of town and you've driven up and down the main street three times, you're stomach's growling, and you're beginning to fear that Goody's has gone out of business. The day I visited Blue Hill, I finally parked in front of the City Building and decided to continue my search on foot. Across the street was an unmarked building, cafe-ish looking but signless. I looked in the window. It was noon and the place was crowded; what else could it be? "Is this Goody's Place?" I asked, feeling a little silly. The jolly waitress behind the counter answered in Nebraska's favorite affirmative, "You bet!" Then she added, "Where you from?"

Goody's is located in the Schumann Building which was built in 1890, right after Blue Hill's big fire. When you walk in you'd swear that things haven't changed much since that day. The unusual tin walls, elaborately decorated, especially stand out.

The food is typical small town cafe: simple and tasty with farmer-size helpings. The kind of place that makes its own pies and peels its own potatoes every morning.

But what I remember most about Goody's was the prices. They made me think that inflation hadn't had much luck finding Blue Hill. I had the special which featured a huge serving of goulash, green beans, mashed potatoes and gravy, watermelon, coffee, and dessert for $3.60. I'm going to return someday for breakfast: two eggs, hash browns, toast, and coffee for one dollar.

Korner Kafe—Byron

402-236-8642

E ntering Byron from the north, I found a deserted implement company. Two blocks to the east a green water tower stood watch over a main street wide enough for four lanes of traffic or for a four-horse team and wagon to turn around. In the middle of the street, a stooped figure in a red Husker jacket walked past another implement dealer, Byron Implement Co. The faded sign out front and the dark windows said it too was out of business. The figure disappeared into a small grocery store. The street for three blocks in each direction was once again deserted. Byron, like many rural communities, showed symptoms of successive years of drought and a decade of shrinking population.

Driving north along the main street, I saw a small brick school, too small to have a gymnasium. The sign out front proclaimed, "Home of the Byron High Broncos." I learned later that it was no longer a high school; now Byron kids go to a consolidated school.

I did a U-turn—few laws and even fewer deputies in Byron—and parked about half way down the main street. At the far end of town stood a tall backdrop of metal grain elevators. At the other end was the former high school. Strung between was the grocery store, a bar, a bank, a rusty metal lawn chair on the sidewalk, a community center, a library, a filling station, two pickups, a '57 Chevy, a sleepy yellow dog, an American flag blowing in the south wind, and the Korner Kafe.

There were no cars in front of the Kafe. I felt that "out-of-business" feeling that I often get these days in small towns. But the sign said "We're Open," so I walked in. I was greeted by a smiling lady in her 60s. At 11 a.m., it was too early for lunch, I thought, but when she said lunch was ready and it was "really good today," my plans for coffee and a roll were abruptly laid aside.

She recommended the broiled pork chop, and I sat down at a freshly set place at a long table for the Byron equivalent of a plowman's lunch. Since I was the only customer there at the time, the service was spectacularly attentive.

"What's the average age of the staff?" I asked. Ruby Harms, a tiny lady less than five feet tall, answered evasively, "We're all over 65." They giggled as she added, "That's as specific as I'm gonna get." The cooks and waitresses laughed at my questions, but answered them as they worked.

I learned that the Kafe is a community-owned, nonprofit venture. In 1976 the town cafe closed and the area citizens organized the Byron Community Association. They purchased an old bar and pool hall and, through volunteer help, converted the building into the Korner Kafe. The townsmen take care of most of the maintenance, but fortunately the cooking and serving is left exclusively to the women who make the outrageous wage of $1.50 per hour.

The food is simple, plainly served, traditional American chow. It's like the cooking that the women's group serves at a small town wedding, golden anniversary, or church supper. Daily specials have "stick to your ribs" substance; there's ham loaf, baked steak, fried chicken, meatloaf, and pork ribs. On Saturdays, it's short-order plus the highlight of the week—fresh baked pies. Each member of the staff brings two to share. The variety and quality will make you feel like a judge at the state fair.

Thirty seconds after I placed my order, a waitress presented me with a selection of salads, one red jello, one orange jello, one tossed. (I chose red Jello). Sixty seconds later my heaping plate of real mashed potatoes and gravy, creamed cabbage, a pork chop and a roll arrived. Where else in the world can you get home-cooked food served at a pace that would put McDonald's to shame?

The pork chop was covered with a delicate golden-brown glaze. The meat was moist and fall-away-from-the-bone tender. The potatoes and cabbage were just as good.

By the time my cake arrived, the place had started to fill. A man in his 90s and a young farmer with his five-year-old daughter sat down across the room. I was joined at the table by Emma Renz, an eighty-eight-year-old mother of eleven who still tends her own garden. Although she no longer works as a volunteer at the restaurant, she explained she was part of the original clean-up staff that fourteen years ago converted the old, grimy bar and pool hall into the Korner Kafe.

The Kafe was almost full when I said goodby to my new friends and walked out into the street. There were ten cars and pickups in front now and two more senior citizens were making their way across the street. Despite deserted buildings, and the advanced ages of its citizens, there's still a lot of life in Byron.

Coney Island Lunch Room—Grand Island

104 East 3rd, 308-382-7155

Germans created the frankfurter, but the Greeks are responsible for the development of the hot dog in America. Take, for example, Constantine "Gus" Poulos, whose famous Papaya King at the corner of 86th Street and Third Avenue in New York City sells three thousand hot dogs a day. Gus's motto for his tube steaks is "tastier than filet mignon." I'm not sure I'd go quite that far, but if one of your favorite eating pleasures is a well-turned frank on a soft bun whose sides are just high enough to handle a slather of mustard, pickle relish, sauerkraut, or any other hot dog helper you care to employ, the Papaya King is one of the best places in the country to find it.

Two thousand miles west of the Papaya another Greek, Gus Katrouzos, has made a name for himself in the hot dog hall of fame. In 1933, Gus Katrouzos's father moved to Grand Island. A few weeks after arriving, he invested his life savings in a long narrow storefront in downtown Grand Island. There he began serving hot dogs, better known as coney islands,

Coney Island
Lunch Room
Grand Island

similar to the ones that had been hawked along the beach at Coney Island in New York as early as 1871. He named his restaurant the Coney Island Lunch Room.

Ten years later Gus took over for his father and the business has continued to thrive as a hot dog palace with a vivid personality. It's a Greek family affair. Although Gus's sister finally retired three years ago, Gus, at sixty-six, is still going strong. The staff today is made up of Gus, wife Christina, and their two grown, college-educated children, George and Katherine.

The sign out front is so faded that the Lunch Room is easy to miss, but ask anyone in town; they've all been there. The forty-one-person capacity is strained at noon as loyal patrons line the long lunch counter and pack the row of booths. A counter seat is the most desirable. Seated there, a customer can watch the family, like square dancers, weave an elaborate dance behind the counter while delivering dog after dog to satisfied customers.

The house specialty, the coney island, is an all-beef weiner nestled in a fresh soft bun. However, it's the topping that sets it off from most civilized dogs. The sauce is a secret spicy chili liberally dolloped over the weiner and then sprinkled with chunks of freshly-sliced onions. Very few customers order only one; the Lunch Room sells about 300 coneys a day, a much higher ratio for the population than the Papaya King in Manhattan.

The Papaya King provides papaya juice to wash down its franks. The Lunch Room offers a classic 1940s-style milk shake. You know how it goes: ice cream, flavoring, and milk are dumped into a huge, shiny canister that mysteriously attaches itself to a whirring green mixer. Then the shake is poured into a large glass which is set before you along with the half-filled metal canister.

Gus is a hoot too. He'll keep you entertained with his constant banter on such topics as the Greek Orthodox church, local politics, or the horse races at Fonner Park. You might also ask him to tell you how the Greeks have revolutionized the American hot dog.

Dreisbach's—Grand Island

1137 South Locust, 308-382-5450

T he world's best steaks are served in the Midwest. It is here that cattle are fed the abundant grain required to produce marbled beef that is tender, succulent, and full of flavor. The large Midwest steakhouses gain the competitive edge in taste by buying whole sides of beef, hanging them in their own coolers during the critical aging process, and cutting them on the premises. Pre-cut, frozen beef just doesn't match up to the fresh, perfectly aged genuine article.

Included among the great steakhouses of our region are the Golden Ox in Kansas City, Mortons in Chicago, and the Buckhorn Exchange in Denver. Johnny's and Ross's of Omaha are up there too. But for real red-meat quality, Dreisbach's in Grand Island is tops. (It was the only Nebraska establishment included in a recent *Midwest Living* list of the top ten steakhouses in the area.)

You can get any kind of steak imaginable at Dreisbach's. It can even be custom cut. A friend from California who hadn't been back to Nebraska in years was determined to eat the biggest steak available. I watched in coronary shock as this beef-starved Californian consumed a custom three-pounder.

Dreisbach's beef is supplemented by a wide variety of specialties. During World War II when beef was scarce, the owner Ferd Dreisbach fed his loyal customers rabbit and chicken, and they still remain a popular item on Dreisbach's menu. Lobster and other seafood are also on the menu.

Along with the entrees come hot baking-powder biscuits and honey, lettuce salad, and your choice of five kinds of homemade dressings. The dressings include a deadly garlic variety that puts you into garlic shock and can keep your spouse away for a solid week. (I always eat a half a jar of it before I go fishing in Minnesota—keeps the mosquitoes away.) Try the sunflower potatoes too—they're a cross between cheesy hashbrowns and crisp potato cakes.

The restaurant originated in 1932 in a two-story farmhouse. Its tradition of farm-style meals continues with heaping plates of all-you-can-eat fried chicken and bowls of mashed potatoes and vegetables.

As in most Nebraska steakhouses, the atmosphere in Dreisbach's is as plain as an I-80 truckstop. The service is usually efficient, although not outstanding. But for beef—the kind that is hard to find outside of the Midwest—Dreisbach's is the place. Dreisbach's is beef lover's heaven.

G.I. Candy Kitchen and Cafe—Grand Island

313 North 3rd, 308-382-7432

T he G.I. Candy Kitchen and Cafe is a museum. It'll take you back, way back in time. In fact, when you step into the Cafe, you're stepping back past your childhood. You're stepping into an antique that has been operating for over eighty years. On the front counter, look at the faded picture of the interior of the cafe (probably taken about 1910); everything's the same as it is now, except for the way the patrons are dressed. When I heard about this place, I was sure reports of its peculiarity were exaggerated. They weren't. When I walked in, I knew I'd found a vintage treasure. On the left was an old soda fountain with a marble counter. On the right was a huge antique display case filled with a wide assortment of homemade candies, including a slab of fudge that could supply every sweet tooth in Grand Island for the next year.

The building is narrow and deep, and the back half is filled with booths of polished cherry wood. The tables are covered with oil cloth. Cherry wainscotting extends halfway up the walls and from there light-green plaster continues to a high, pressed-tin ceiling in pastel pink. There is an ancient jukebox, probably the youngest thing in the place, except for the gregarious, fifty-something waitress. Hanging on the jukebox is a hand-lettered sign: "If the lights on this Box are not on, Don't put your Money in. Thanks, the Management."

The prices on the menu are also antique. A hamburger deluxe, $1.20, cheese ten cents extra. I ordered chili and the house specialty, a burger. I found the chili below average; but tastes can change. Perhaps the recipe won a prize at a 1910 cook-off. The hamburger, however, was excellent. It reminded me of the burgers of my childhood, obviously fried on a grill with plenty of grease for flavor. Even the bun had that old-fashioned greasy feel. The meal was hard on the arteries, but when they served them like this eighty years ago, nobody knew any better.

On the way out I stopped at the candy counter and bought a bag of dark chocolate-covered marshmallows. I was going to ration them, but the candy, like the sweetness of childhood, was gone before I knew it.

Nonna's Palazzo—Grand Island

820 West 2nd, 308-384-3029

Nonna's is a true American dream. Chiarra Brazzale, the restaurant's namesake, grew up in Vincentaza, Italy, where she dreamed of coming to America. In 1914 her dream came true, and she immigrated to the United States, landing in Sunrise, Wyoming, where she set up a boarding house. Most of her roomers were Italian men who worked in the iron mines nearby, and she cooked hearty food from the old country to please these lonely workers.

Chiarra Brazzale's grandaughter, Fran Schaffer, used to visit her nonna (Italian for grandmother) in Wyoming. While working with her during these visits, Fran learned the secrets of Italian cooking.

Like her nonna, Fran also had a dream. Growing up in Grand Island, Fran and her brother would often walk by what they considered the most magnificient home in the world, the Hamilton-Donald House. "It was the only house in Grand Island that I ever wanted," she says. "It was so majestic looking." When she was in the third grade, she nearly asked the owner if she could buy the house. She had fifty cents.

In 1983, Fran's own dream came true. She and her husband purchased the house and moved their family into the upstairs rooms. Fran retired from nursing and fulfilled the rest of her dream—to carry on the Italian cooking tradition inspired by her grandmother.

She named her restaurant Nonna's Palazzo. Palazzo means "palace," and the name fits for the house is a mansion. Built in 1905 by banker Ellsworth D. Hamilton, the three-story white house is an example of the neo-classic revival style. Listed in the National Register of Historic Places, it has a full height portico supported by eight large wooden columns crowned with Corinthian capitals. The house features lavish stained and leaded glass as well as ornate woodwork.

Meals are served in the living room to the left of the foyer as you enter and in the dining room to the right. The furnishings are antique pieces that Fran has collected over the years. The elegant atmosphere is even further enhanced with soft classical music in the background.

Fran is the only cook and from the quality of her fare, it is clear that her nonna was a great tutor. State-of-the-art pasta, homemade from bleached flour, is the house specialty. For lunch the day I visited I had lemon chicken with fettuccini. It was magnifico, as were the homemade dinner rolls, homemade ice cream and the dessert of chantilly (a meringue shell filled with strawberries). When I go back I'm going to try the sour cream raisin pie. Of course, if I happen to be there on a Tuesday or Wednesday, I'll have to have coconut cream pie; if I'm there on a Thursday or Friday, I must sample the chocolate angel food cake.

The new menu designates low-cholesterol selections and includes daily specials. The regular items are mainly the non-spicy northern Italian variety. There is pasta galore: spaghetti, fettuccine, raviola, lasagna, and Italian T-bone steak. In spite of the gourmet quality and the elegance of the surroundings, you'll be amazed at the reasonable prices. The lunch plates are only $4.95 and the platters (designed for the likes of iron workers and me) only $5.95. Dinners range from $8 to $13.

Going to Nonna's is like being invited to someone's home, but not just anybody's home; the atmosphere and the Italian cooking at Nonna's are special. Like Nonna and Fran, I dream: of returning to Nonna's.

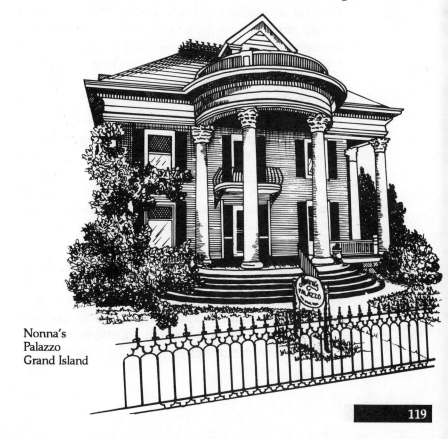

Nonna's
Palazzo
Grand Island

402-284-2217

Some people say location is the most important factor in the restaurant business. If this is true, Debby Fischer and mother Ruth McClatchy must love a challenge. They've had the courage to start a cafe in a place that sounds more like a mantra for meditation than a village. Ong is almost a ghost town. All that's left is a grain elevator, a filling station, and the Country Village Cafe. Not only is Ong a lonely place, but the county in which it sits has only 8,000 potential customers spread thinly over 576 square miles.

In spite of such isolation, these ladies forged ahead. Like walkers in a wheatfield, they were determined to go against the grain. And, if location isn't enough of a problem, they decided to stray from the typical meatloaf and mashed potato fare of country cafes. They weren't content to fill stomachs. These women wanted to educate palates.

It's true that they pack the house on Sunday with conventional fried chicken coated in a copyrighted breading–that Mrs. McClatchy markets, along with a special steak marinade, around the state. On other days, however, creativity reigns. They serve chicken in white wine sauce, steaks grilled southwestern style over a mesquite fire, barbequed ribs, and a variety of Mexican dishes.

The Cafe is located in a type of metal building used frequently for garages, cattle sheds, and implement businesses. However, the inside has been cozied up a bit with country crafts so that you almost forget that you're eating coq au vin in a metal building. But don't fret about atmosphere, the food makes up for it.

One word of warning: I'd advise going for lunch only, preferably Sunday lunch. When I've dropped in for an evening meal, there was a substitute chef. Unfortunately, he told me that he only serves things he can heat up in the microwave.

The Big Idea—Sutton

402-773-4321

Most people own a restaurant to make a living, but when you sit in the Big Idea watching its owner, Bev Griess, cook in her open kitchen, you get the impression that she owns a restaurant so she can do something different everyday. And that's just what she cooks—something different everyday. She keeps 'em guessing in Sutton. On one day the special may be Spanish, on the next, German or Swedish. Who knows, tomorrow she may be introducing the Sutton palates to Moroccan couscous or chilled Bulgarian cucumber soup.

Sometimes her customers ask: "Bev, what do you call this red stuff?" But whatever she calls it, they usually love it. Bev Griess is a cooking fiend whose foible is her inability to avoid trying out new recipes on her willing guinea pigs . . . rather, her willing and appreciative customers.

The Big Idea has no menu. That would be too predictable. It has only a monthly paper placemat listing daily specials. This is supplemented by a chalk board behind the counter displaying Bev's current culinary whims. Her whims include the standard Nebraska offerings of pork, beef, and chicken, but she prefers to transform these basic meats with the magic of a wild variety of seasonings, sauces, and combinations. Here's a brief sample of this lady's imagination: chicken strata, barbecue steak, German croissant, pork feather bones, and fruit pizza.

Only on Friday does she show any degree of conformity. Obviously exhausted by another week of cooking creativity, she reluctantly puts out the soup, salad, and sandwich bar. But don't expect to be able to guess the kind of soup, salad or sandwich. That, too, is different every week.

The day I was there she served scalloped chicken on pasta, green beans, a marinated fruit cup, pumpkin pie, and coffee for $3.25. The food was good, but most importantly it was a pleasant change from what you would normally expect for lunch in a small main street cafe.

Oh yes, don't go into the Big Idea expecting to order a hamburger or french fries. She doesn't serve such conventional fare. If she doesn't throw you out, she'll undoubtedly suggest you go to the nearest McDonald's to get something that will taste the same everytime you eat it. Don't ever accuse Bev Griess of homogenizing America's taste. To the contrary, her cooking gently diverts her patrons away from routine, boring food and leads them on an eating adventure. She summarizes her cooking philosophy: "There's more to eating than hamburgers."

Nebraska's Eating Oddities

An Essay

Everyone's writing a cookbook these days. The ability to cook isn't even a prerequisite. Even the governor's husband has published a cookbook, and you can just guess how often he cooks.

My credentials for a cookbook venture include a stint at cooking school. Granted it wasn't exactly the Cordon Bleu in France, but it was cooking, and it was in school: I took Home Ec for Boys in high school. In fact, I got one of my best grades in that class, a C plus. Home Ec for Boys, which the girls called Remedial Homemaking, was the start of my lifelong love of cooking—other people's cooking.

The cookbook I put together will be different. No French recipes, no cream sauces, nothing so ordinary. In fact, the recipes in my cookbook may not be edible by current standards. My cookbook will be called *Nebraska Eating Oddities*, and it will be about bizarre combinations of foods that Nebraskans have stomached over the decades. Fortunately for you, I don't have the time nor space here to include detailed recipes, but I'd like to give you a preview of my cookbook. I guarantee the authenticity of this material. No matter how revolting you might consider it, its source is the writings of some of the top culinary historians of the Plains.

Native American Fare: The first Americans, of course, didn't have supermarkets. Thus, they had to make do with what they could find. Their tastes were as wide ranging as their foraging. While the French were dining on shallots, squid, truffles, and snails, Native Americans matched them bite for bite with ant soup (the ants were scooped up from anthills in the cool of the morning, washed, crushed to a paste, and mixed with water); dried, boiled, or roasted grasshoppers; beaver tails (cut into small slices and boiled with prairie turnips until very tender); wild peas (robbed from the caches of field mice and boiled with fat buffalo meat); chokecherries and rose pods (pounded and mixed with bone grease); and boiled dog (seasoned with bark). (Courtesy of Ian Frazier, *Great Plains*.)

Native cooking methods have also been documented. Historian E.T. Denig contributes this recipe for Christmas goose: "Smear over the goose a thick coat of mud (this is over the goose as it is killed with the feathers, entrails, and everything intact). Then the bird is put in a hot fire and covered over with live coals. Here it is left until the clay covering becomes red hot, then allowed to cool gradually until the fire dies out. The shell is then cracked with an ax, the feathers and skin of the goose come off with the clay, leaving the flesh clean and well done." This recipe is not recommended for the small modern kitchen. It's difficult to take a full backswing with an ax in such places.

Pemmican, an early day K ration, was made by combining equal parts of buffalo suet, dried fruit, and some type of game, often venison. The mixture was formed into bricks and then dried in the sun. These bricks, which must have resembled my Aunt Mabel's homemade bread-doorstops, were consumed in chunks or bitten off on the run. The bricks could also be immersed in water to make a thick soup or stew. Kay Graber's *Nebraska Pioneer Cookbook* gives you more detailed information than you may want to know about such food.

> Pemmican, an early day K ration, was made by combining equal parts of buffalo suet, dried fruit, and some type of game, often venison.

Of course, Plains Indians ate lots of buffalo. Delicacies included buffalo paunch and buffalo blood boiled with brains, rosebuds, and hide scrapings. (Frazier again.)

Cowboy Chow: Nebraska cowboys didn't get much home cookin'. They were at the mercy of the outfit's cook who was usually a crotchety old cowboy too stove up to handle his range duties any more. Most likely, the "cook" received all his culinary training atop a bucking bronc. The cowhands used to say that the best seasoning for the camp cook's chow was a salty sense of humor. (Alsted, *Savvy Sayin's.*)

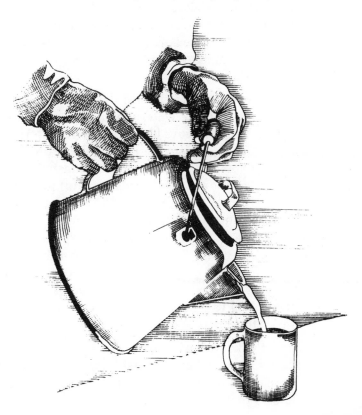

Hygiene was probably not his first concern. For example, a rancher's daughter, along on a short drive, complained to the cook that he didn't even wash his hands when he baked the bread. The cook replied indignantly: "Why I do too wash 'em. How'd I ever get the dough offen 'em if I didn't?" (Stan Hoig, *The Humor of the American Cowboy.*)

Three cowboy recipes stand out—crisped marrow gut, mountain oysters, and horseshoe coffee. Crisped marrow gut is made from the narrow passageway between the two main stomachs of the cow. This gut, which contains a substance resembling bone marrow, is cut into pieces about one and a half inches in length and then deep-fat-fried in a skillet until nearly crisp. Then you remove and salt it, pour off the fat, and return the marrow-gut to the skillet to keep warm until you eat it.

Most cowboys claimed that cooks were much too generous with the water when it came to making good coffee. Yup, cowboys liked their coffee strong. They often said, "The grub in this outfit is a mite weak tastin', but the coffee is strong enuf to bring up the average." (Alsted again.) It was said that six cups of town coffee equalled one cup of cowboy coffee. Here's the famous horsehoe recipe for strong coffee. Add two pounds of coffee to two gallons of boiling water. Boil two hours, then throw in a horseshoe. If it sinks, the coffee isn't done.

> Add two pounds of coffee . . . . Boil two hours, then throw in a horseshoe. If it sinks, the coffee isn't done.

Rocky Mountain oysters are the testicles of bull calves, removed during castration. Although the squeamish won't touch them, the oyster aficionado knows that they are one of the world's great delicacies.

Also known as prairie oysters and bull fries, they are sliced about one and a half inches thick and deep-fat fried. The resulting crisp-crusted disks have a soft texture that is delicate and extremely rich. Some cowpokes claimed they were an aphrodisiac, but these fellows had just been in the saddle too long.

Pioneer Grub: Not to be outdone, the settlers came up with some strange combinations too. I am fond of the way the name of the dish phonetically matches the end product. Some old standbys were samp (fresh-plucked yellow corn crushed then boiled and served with syrup or milk), souse (pickled pig's feet), and sheep's pluck (the liver and lungs baked with potatoes and onions, casserole-style). I could go on and on, but I'll conclude with two of my favorites, peach leather and corn cob syrup. Peach leather is boiled sugar and peaches mashed to a paste and then spread out on a platter to dry in the sun. Roll up the dried layer in a muslin cloth and store it in a cool place. To eat, simply unroll the cloth and tear off pieces. Corn cob syrup is made with a dozen large, red corn cobs. Boil the cobs for two hours, preferably after you've shaken the dust off. Add brown sugar to the cob water and boil to the desired thickness. Great on flapjacks.

> Any Nebraska bartender who hesitates when you order red beer is an Oklahoma spy.

The Nebraska tradition of odd concoctions continues. First, there's red beer. It's four parts beer to one part tomato juice. It settles the fizz in the beer and makes yuppie out-of-staters think they're drinking something truly exotic. Any Nebraska bartender who hesitates when you order red beer is an Oklahoma spy. And how about Nebraska corn nuggets, invented at the Pool Hall in Eustis: they are a single kernel of creamed corn encased in a fried batter. They're about the size of a marble. Try them. If you don't like em, they're great sling-shot ammo. Then there is an eastern import which has crept into the state—buffalo wings (no, Plains buffaloes don't have wings). These are spicy, barbecued chicken wings invented in Buffalo, New York. These wings are sprouting in taverns all over the state, but some hope they'll soon take flight. Finally, there's toasted ravioli, rolled in flour and deep-fat fried. The only place I've found this is at Mr. C's in Omaha.

This list of peculiar edibles proves that Nebraskans will eat just about anything. As for the cookbook idea, I think I'll make it a diet cookbook. Some of these recipes take my appetite away just writing about them.

Significant Others—South Central

Ole Panhandler—Beaver City
308-268-5144

Antique farm equipment decorates this restaurant in the area that gave rise to Senator George Norris and Kool-Aid (invented in nearby Hendley). Humongous salad bar on Saturday nights; reservations suggested. Scaled-down salad bar accompanies prime rib and crab legs on Fridays. For something different, there's buffalo steak on Thursdays.

Conoco Cafe —Grand Island
2109 West 2nd
308-382-9621

Gas up while you eat—big pot of baked beans is a regular feature. Truck-stop-style cafe for cars only (no parking for 18 wheelers). Plain old Midwest meals that'll top off your tank at self-serve prices.

The Front Porch—Hastings
402-463-7117

You've never seen this much food on a front porch. The buffet island (too big to be called a bar), surrounded by front porches, would keep a stranded sailor alive for years. It has it all—onion rings, great slabs of cheese, Mexican and Italian fixin's, every conceivable salad item, and desserts. The day I was there they also had shrimp and crab legs. A nicely decorated family restaurant with enough food to feed regiments.

LoRaynes—Hastings
402-463-2784

Go to LoRaynes hungry; the salad bar and entree buffet will still even the fiercest stomach growl. Country cooking in all-you-can-eat quantities.

Sportsman's Corner Steakhouse —Nelson
402-225-3581

A haven for baseball fans, even without hot-dogs on the menu. The big draw is a display of memorabilia from hometown hero, Russ Snyder, late of the Orioles. Every wall is covered with highly collectible, autographed pictures, bats, and pennants (even from the Washington Senators). If you have to eat after savoring the souvenirs, the steaks will be a big hit, maybe even a home run.

Little Mexico—Republican City
308-799-3205

Mexican food plays to standing-room-only crowd on the weekends. Huge margaritas for starters (after that everything else tastes great). Two large enchiladas for $1.85 (that's only a half order). Sensational sopapillas.

Strang Tavern—Strang
402-759-4834

Located in heart of the Strang-Ong-Edgar metroplex of south central Nebraska, the tavern sits on the site of the Strang Opera House destroyed by fire in 1930. Woodsy decor, hunters' trophies, and historic photographs of the opera house. Its claim to fame is a large hamburger called the Strang Supreme, rated by some as one of the top burgers in the state: ground beef covered with cheese, mushrooms, and Canadian bacon.

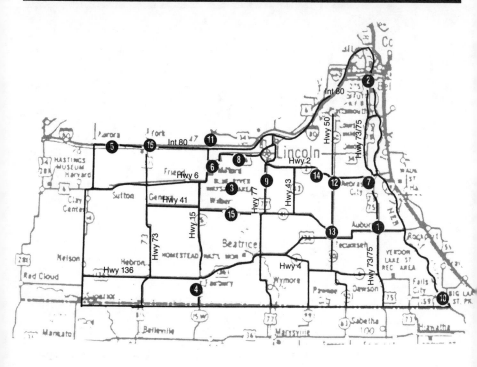

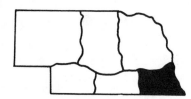

Southeast

1. Auburn—Arbor Manor
2. Bellevue—Nettie's
3. Crete—Heidi and Harold's
   Winners
4. Fairbury—Courtyard Square
5. Henderson—Dutch Kitchen
6. Milford—Kup 'n Kettle
7. Nebraska City—Ulbrick's
8. Pleasant Dale—Rudy and Marlene's
9. Princeton—Princeton Tavern
10. Rulo—Camp Rulo River Club
11. Seward—Our House
12. Syracuse—Caroline's Coffee Shop
13. Tecumseh—Helen's Cafe
14. Unadilla—Horstmans
15. Wilber—Club Wilber
16. York—Chances R

Eating in the Darndest Places

Years ago Nebraskans filled their stomachs at campfires, in dark and musty soddies, and in raucous saloons. Things haven't changed all that much. We still eat just about any place we can—stables, Victorian houses, machine sheds, lumber yards, bookie joints, vegetable warehouses, hardware stores, mortuaries, jewelry stores, and banks. Nebraska eateries, in addition to satisfying our appetites, have provided a second chance for many such buildings. Here are a few examples:

Ulbrick's Cafe, Nebraska City. This restaurant offers "all-you-can-eat" family-style meals in a converted service station. When the food comes, it doesn't make any difference whether you're in the old grease pit or the dining room; the pan-fried chicken is good enough for heaven. Don't overeat, though; this former filling station, can still give you gas.

> Once a mortuary, now it's a lively restaurant, and the customers are still dying to get in.

K.C.'s Emporium, Fremont. Once a mortuary, now it's a lively restaurant, and the customers are still dying to get in.

Barrymore's, Lincoln. Jim Haberlan, a Lincoln architect, created Barrymore's Lounge out of the backstage of the old Stuart Theatre. The movie screen is just opposite the bar's north wall, and on quiet nights, a loud movie soundtrack can be heard through the wall. Any flick of the car chase, shoot-em-up, slash-and-gash, horror genre can make an otherwise quiet evening pretty exhilarating.

Little Diner Cafe, Ulysses. When I ate at the Little Diner Cafe in Ulysses years ago, Ruth Vandeberge, the seventy-three-year-old proprietor, provided a detailed history of the building. First it was a drug store, then a feed store, next a creamery, and then a harness shop. "Finally," she reported, "it's my diner." Sad to say, now even the diner is gone.

Rudy and Marlene's Tavern, Pleasant Dale. This former bank was the scene of a robbery in 1903 when three robbers blew the safe and escaped with $3500. The hard times of the depression spelled the end of the bank, and for at least the last thirty years it's been the town tavern. The beer is cold and the burgers are good—you can still bank on it.

> First it was a drug store, then a feed store, next a creamery, and then a harness shop. "Finally," she reported, "it's my diner."

Roosevelt's, Grand Island (Rest in Peace). Roosevelt's was located in the former library. Everyone knows you're not supposed to eat in a library, and who wants to whisper through an entire meal. For these reasons, Roosevelt's demise, like my last library book, was long overdue.

Marilyn's Tea Room, Beemer. The main floor of this cozy, old Victorian home is a terrific place for lunch. After a huge meal, I wanted to crawl upstairs for a nap.

Courtyard Square, Fairbury. A skillful decorator has converted this former Montgomery Ward store into a surprisingly classy restaurant. I ate in an area formerly occupied by the lingerie department, but the food wasn't flimsy.

Beef 'n Stuff, Page. Previously a machine shop, Beef 'n Stuff can repair sagging energy with healthy food light on the grease and oil.

Neligh House, West Point. Leading to the upstairs bar is an elegant staircase and banister from the old St. Joseph's Hospital in Omaha. But the food at Neligh House fortunately bears no resemblance to hospital fare.

Kup 'n Kettle, Milford. Located in a former auto dealership, the Kup 'n Kettle is a place you can't af-Ford to miss.

Heidi and Harold's—Crete

123 East 13th, 402-826-9932

I'd never eaten Czech food before I went to the Wilber Czech Festival where I tried roast pork, sauerkraut, and dumplings. It was love at first bite. I then began thinking about how good it was and wished I could have some more before Czech Days rolled around again. Sound familiar? Fortunately, I finally discovered a way to control my newly created craving for Czech food—Heidi and Harold's Cafe in Crete.

Although Katherine and I live only twelve miles from Crete, I always assumed Heidi and Harold's was a Swiss restaurant. Not so. Friday and Saturday evenings every other weekend the restaurant offers authentic Czech fare. The specialties are roast duck and roast pork. Both are good, but the last time I was there, I chose the pork, thick tender slices of it served on dressing and smothered with gravy. Also included is rye bread and best of all, spicy and vinegary sauerkraut with caraway seed. Starters were a small salad and liver dumpling soup, something similar to chicken noodle but with liver dumplings. I had the traditional kolaches for dessert.

Not exactly the Pritikin diet, but it must not hurt you because I know a lot of long-lived Czechs in Crete and Wilber. Perhaps it's because they get so much sleep; sleep is the only thing you can do after eating a meal like that.

On other days of the week H and H's is a typical small town cafe with good food, and plenty of it at small town prices.

Kup 'n Kettle—Milford

604 1st St., 402-761-2442

T he closest thing to a stampede that has happened in Nebraska since the invention of barbed wire is the herd of Milford folks rushing to the Kup 'n Kettle on Saturday morning. The first time I stopped in for some early morning nourishment, I hadn't heard how worked up the natives get about the fresh-baked donuts, rolls, and pastries. I discovered that standing by the front door jawing with a friend at that time of day is about as safe as riding a bicycle in a buffalo herd. That might be exaggerating a bit, but it wouldn't be exaggerating to report that by the time I managed to make it safely into a booth for breakfast, the line of hungry folks stretched from the bakery counter clear across the room to the front door. In fact, the first time I was there most of the baked goods were sold by 9:30 a.m..I made the mistake of waiting until after breakfast to order pecan rolls for the trip home. "Sorry but they're all gone, my waitress replied. "Try to get here a little earlier next week or at least buy your baked goods before you have breakfast." This is the first bakery I've tried that could require reservations.

Two sisters, Darla Armstrong and Cheryl Hostetler, started the Kup about two years ago. And they say they never experienced the slow start-up period that most restaurants must weather. The staff is friendly, and in addition to the great breakfasts, the place is packed for the lunch specials, too, including two or three homemade soups each day. And for dessert, how about raspberry chiffon pie or chocolate peanut pie? Unfortunately, it's closed for dinner. (Maybe that's why everyone is so hungry by breakfast time.)

From the way they've decorated the place, you'd never know it's the former home of Milford Motors. So for food that will really rev your engine, I recommend the Kup 'n Kettle. But get there early and don't tarry at the front door.

Ulbrick's Cafe—Nebraska City

402-873-5458

I'd been driving since dawn, playing leapfrog with eighteen-wheelers, looking for ways to get around pokey motorhomes, and stopping only long enough to take on gas and visit the restroom. After a skimpy breakfast, I'd skipped lunch, except for diet pop and a bag of popcorn. Now it was almost five thirty in the evening. I was road weary and hungry, but I knew my craving wouldn't be satisfied by a national hamburger factory. I needed food, I needed food fast (not fast food), and above all I needed lots of it. Glancing at my map, I felt like a nomad who had just spotted an oasis—the next spot on the map read Nebraska City, home of Ulbrick's Cafe.

I called ahead for a reservation and to place my order. (Most Sundays you can forget it if you don't have a reservation.) After taking my reservation, the lady asked, "And you want the chicken?" Just about everyone orders the chicken. Charlene Chapin, founder Mary Ulbrick's daughter, still cooks it the way her mom did—no batter, fried with lard in an old-fashioned skillet with only flour for crust. They also offer steaks, ham, and shrimp, but I suggest you stick with the chicken.

Ulbrick's is located in a converted filling station. The extra plain down-home decor of the main kitchen and dining room doesn't resemble the former business, but a few feet to the north is the garage that used to house the grease rack. As I walked in the front door, I was greeted by a junior-high maitre d' in jeans, teeshirt, and basketball shoes. He was enthusiastic and pleasant as he showed me to a plastic-covered table already set with the first two bowls of food—spicy sauerkraut slaw and a tapioca-marshmallow-citrus whip (ambrosia). What a combination!

As I walked in, I could see Charlene's face framed in the large hole cut into the kitchen behind the counter. Stationed in that strategic spot, just as her mother Mary had been for so many years, she directs the kitchen and her well-trained and efficient young staff just like a ship's captain.

After I devoured the first two offerings, the waiter brought on the fried chicken and family-style bowls of lettuce salad, green beans, french fries, creamed corn, creamed cabbage, thick homemade noodles, and rolls. Any emptied bowls, except for the chicken platter, were quickly replaced with fresh-filled ones. When I came up for air, I again told myself that Ulbrick's is nothing fancy, but it is tasty, calorie-packed, basic belly-filling food that is bound to satisfy. After sampling the homemade pies (made with pure lard), and purchasing Mary's $1 cookbook (which contains her "secrets of cooking," pictures of her grandchildren, and such helpful hints as "carrots peeled under warm water will not leave stain on the hands"), I waddled out of Ulbrick's. As I loosened my seatbelt, I knew I wouldn't eat again for a week. Hunger pangs only a distant memory, I wheeled on down the road.

Rudy and Marlene's Tavern—Pleasant Dale

402-795-9915

T he former First State Bank Building in Pleasant Dale, now Rudy and Marlene's Tavern, has had an interesting past. Built in 1901, the red brick building served as Pleasant Dale's bank until the depression swept it out of business.

The building's most exciting event occurred on October 20, 1903, when the citizens were jarred out of bed at 4 a.m. by a blast that was said to shake every house in town. As the townspeople rushed out of their homes, they saw a huge cloud of smoke pouring out of the bank. "They've blowed the safe. Get your guns, boys," somebody yelled. A getaway buggy was spotted heading west out of town. The night-shirted posse grabbed their guns and raced barefoot across a stubble field. By cutting across the field, they were able to get close enough to spray the fleeing buggy with a volley of bullets. The buggy stopped. The posse rushed up, guns cocked, ready for more heroic action. The driver thrust quivering arms high in surrender. His face, pale in the moonlit night, looked familiar. Slowly a women and three frightened children arose from the floor boards. Instead of desperate bank robbers, the bullet-riddled buggy contained the terrified, but unharmed family of local farmer George Mundhenke. The Mundhenkes had been returning from a visit to relatives when the blast startled their horses. Later it was learned that the real robbers left town by a different road. The $3500 stolen that night was never recovered (and after that experience, the Mundhenkes always returned home before dark.)

By the time I came to the Pleasant Dale area in the early sixties, the bank had served as a barber shop, a credit union, and a post office. In 1963 it was a tavern called the Flying Key. The north wall had a huge map of the United States with motel keys from all across the nation hung in the appropriate locations.

The tavern's name has changed several times, but it's most distinctive architectural feature remains. The ceiling is covered with multi-colored egg cartons, and is perhaps the only bar ceiling of its kind in existence. (At least that's what I tell everyone.)

I've had some good times in there, particularly on Sunday afternoons when country western bands played. It was common to see neighbor ladies dancing with each other (while men played cards and pool) or three-year-olds learning to dance by the trial-and-error method. You could sit in there on a Sunday afternoon sipping a few brews, watching the kids run around like wild goats, and humming along to such favorite tunes as "Courtin' in the Rain" and "I Was Lookin' Back to See If You Was Lookin' Back at Me." Mondays didn't seem so bad after that.

The food has never been anything more than Midwest prairie grub—burgers, fries, and such—but it all tasted good in the company of friends. The present owners continue to keep the beer cold and the bar's pickled sausage jar full. Business has picked up since the management started daily specials like three tacos for $1.50 on Tuesdays and mountain oysters on Wednesdays. It ain't fancy, but it's home.

Princeton Tavern—Princeton

402-798-9950

J ust south of Lincoln on Highway 77 is the Ivy League of Mexican cuisine, the Princeton Tavern. This little cantina packs them in for homemade Mexican food on Thursday through Saturday nights. The short drive makes a great family outing, and on the night I visited, more than half the patrons were under twelve years old. Mom and Dad can enjoy a margarita while waiting for the food to arrive, and the kids can find plenty of fun with a pool table, video games, and what looks like a small dance floor to run around. Throughout the restaurant, small siblings and strangers mingled under the watchful gaze of adults, just like the taverns of old. The jukebox pounds, and time stands still.

The Princeton Tavern is a pleasant place to linger. It's reminiscent of a 50s-style rec room with knotty-pine walls, and a linoleum floor. Large plate glass windows along the east wall make the atmosphere brighter and more inviting than most dark, smoky bars. And an enclosed grassy patio is soon to come, making a perfect spot to let loose all those kids.

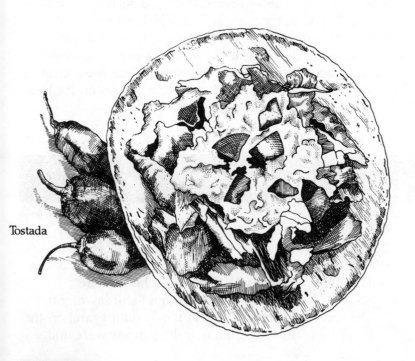

Tostada

The usual tavern decor dominates. There are at least seventy-five signs advertising various beers, and perhaps twice as many different kinds of beer cans perch on shelves around the dining room, evidence of a very serious collector.

The food, however, is the real drawing card, for the Tavern is one of southeast Nebraska's best sources of Mexican food. The food may be anglicized, but the beans-and-rice are tasty, the sauces appropriately spicy, and the portions very generous. The combination dinner—beans, rice, an enchilada, a taco, and a tostada—actually filled two enormous platters. The bean-and-meat stuffed burrito dinner with beans and rice was almost more than I could eat. Homemade chips and salsa, both red and green, complemented the entrees. The sopapillas looked great, but no one had room left to give them a try.

Camp Rulo River Club—Rulo

402-245-4096

Oregon has its salmon, Maine has its lobster, Maryland has its crab, Nebraska has . . . catfish and carp. And one of the best places in Nebraska for catfish and carp is the Camp Rulo River Club. Located on the Nebraska side of the Missouri River in the extreme southeast corner of the state, Camp Rulo may be Nebraska's fried fish capital.

The current eatery is a reincarnation of the original Camp Rulo, a rustic old place cantilevered out over the Missouri. Unfortunately, the original burned down a few years ago, and in its place is a spanking new building built next to the river. The view isn't spectacular, but the surroundings are a lot cleaner.

And the menu is also much the same as the old Camp Rulo: typical rural road-house fare with an emphasis on fish. I have tried both the catfish and the carp there. Although the carp was better than I expected, I much preferred the catfish. The fish is cooked with a light batter in fresh cooking oil. The white meat of the catfish was juicy and tender. It's as fresh as fish gets—they buy it from local fishermen daily. They talk about great seafood in the East, but Missouri River catfish is vastly underrated.

My table by one of the large windows that look out over the river was a pleasant place to pass the time too. It wasn't an ocean view, but it was relaxing to watch the river lazily roll by as I ate.

The dining area is a barnlike room. The only memorable feature is an exhibit of an unusual art form that seems to be gaining popularity in Nebraska—I call it Saw Art, painting done on the blade of a saw. It's folk art that has appeal at flea markets and festivals. It allows for a wide variety of shapes and sizes, and maintains some use if it ever outlives its aesthetic value. The juxtaposition of a mountain landscape on a bucksaw blade can have a sharp effect upon the senses. (A few weeks before my visit an excellent example of a chainsaw painting was shown and received favorable reviews from the patrons, but with winter coming on, the artist withdrew it from exhibit.)

To really know Nebraska, a supper scout must make the trek to Rulo for a night at Camp.

Our House—Seward

217 South 4th, 402-643-6787

The newest owners of this converted Queen-Anne-style house/restaurant hope that the third time's the charm. The attractive small house, just a block off the courthouse square, has been home to three different restaurants in recent years. First it was the Sugar Shack, then PJ's Sugar Shack. After our visit on a busy Friday night, I think the latest incarnation, Our House, is going to be a survivor.

Our House
Seward

Our House is a mom-and-pop operation run by an Iowa couple with restaurant experience. It's truly a family affair: their daughter is a hostess and a grandson sometimes clears tables. The food is strictly down-home, and the prices are unbelievably low for the quantity and quality. It's everything you'd expect in a restaurant named Our House.

Katherine and I had a pork loin and a ham steak; both were just fine. The entrees came with a choice of potato, vegetable, salad, and roll. We topped it off with two slices of pie—coconut cream and strawberry rhubarb—good enough for Grandma to serve to company.

When you're next in Seward, come to Our House for a real family meal.

Caroline's Coffee Shop—Syracuse

454 5th St., 402-269-3251

Caroline's Coffee Shop is as all-American as the great apple pies baked by Alyce Malliard, the sole owner, waitress, chief cook, and bottle washer of this postage-stamp size diner. Alyce, a woman of indeterminate age, has been in the restaurant business for forty-three years. She started working at her mother's place (also named Caroline's) when she was in the ninth grade.

Alyce loves cats and her restaurant features a feline theme. There is a creaky black-cat wall clock with blinking eyes and a tail that moves like a pendulum. Pictures of cats line the walls. The quaint, flea market theme includes a battered oak counter, a lava lamp, a curved-glass pie case, louvered shades, and shelves displaying owls, more cats, a pheasant, and pink plastic flowers. Seating is limited to twelve round metal stools at the counter.

The nostalgia of Caroline's is enough to warrant a visit, but Alyce and her home-cookin are a delightful bonus. Open only for breakfast (homemade rolls with a cinnamon-apple topping the specialty) and lunch (strictly sandwiches, soup and pie), Caroline's main attraction is a big burger that's too big for its homemade bun. "That's something you don't get very many places. I betcha," Alyce claims.

Alyce assured me she's not ready to retire, but said she's the only employee, so keep this place under your hat; she couldn't handle a deluge of eaters wanting to sample her homemade apple pie.

Significant Others—Southeast

Arbor Manor—Auburn
1617 Central Avenue
402-274-3663

Steakhouse fare in the anachronistic atmosphere of a Queen-Anne-style mansion.

Nettie's— Bellevue
7110 Railroad Avenue
402-733-3359

Take along a fire extinguisher and a tough stomach to this Mexican restaurant. The sizzling hot chili will test your tongue and your toughness, but like all the items on the menu, it's authentic, fresh, made from scratch, and delicious. Natividad (Nettie) Escamilla has been cooking great Mexican food for years and it shows. In addition to the chili, some of my favorites are a huge (all the servings are huge) plate of nachos (including homemade flour chips), the Special Toad, a tortilla filled with a concoction of beef, beans, and chili, and Nettie's combos of the usual Mexican specialties.

Don't go for the atmosphere. Instead you'll find elbow-to-elbow happy eaters in this small, popular cantina. Nettie's is probably the best of the authentic Mexican spots in Omaha.

Winners—Crete
1217 Main
402-826-3999

Nothing like the thrill of gambling to aid digestion. At the new Winners in Crete you can play keno while you eat. It was fun and the food was good, but my meal was twice as expensive as usual. Guess I'm an unlucky eater.

Courtyard Square—Fairbury
500 Fourth Street
402-729-3388

A Montgomery Ward store transformed into a surprisingly upscale restaurant. You order off the menu, not from a catalog: party rooms occupy the former lingerie department. Scratch cooking from steak and pork cordon bleu to diet-busting pastries. Mobil Travel Guide rated.

The Dutch Kitchen—Henderson
402-723-5218

They don't serve Dutch food at the Dutch
Kitchen in Henderson, but they do serve
some of the best German food in the state. I
was there on a cold winter evening in
February and the place was packed. The
house specialty, available everyday, is a dish
called verenika, a dough pocket filled with cottage cheese and eggs and smothered with
gravy. It's a downright homely concoction,
the kind I used to avoid as a kid. But dig in.
The taste is unusual, hearty, and much, much
better than it looks. Other German specials
are available each day.

Helen's Cafe—Tecumseh
402-335-3457

One view of the town square in Tecumseh
and it's easy to see why it was chosen as the
location for the ABC-TV miniseries,
"Amerika." Quaint, beautifully restored buildings surround the courthouse, a magnificent
trophy in the center of the town.

Nestled among these buildings is Helen's
Cafe. It's a long-time Tecumseh institution
strongly supported by area residents. I visited
there one Saturday at 7:45 a.m. and it seemed
as though the entire village had come in for
breakfast. The food, tasty and reliable, ranks
up there with the best small-town cafes in the
state. It's an idyllic spot to enjoy genuine Midwest cuisine.

Horstman's Cafe—Unadilla
402-828-5945

Nebraska's most authentic-looking small-
town cafe. Producers of ABC-TV miniseries
"Amerika" borrowed most of furnishings for a
set. Horstman's also starred in political com-
mercials for Senator Bob Kerrey. Food is plentiful and cheap (20% of what a breakfast
would cost in a New York hotel). Quality can
vary from "whoops" to "whoopee," depending on who's running the grill.

Club Wilber—Wilber
402-821-2330

Hardworking owners are always on the
scene here—and it shows. Lowell Kotas is a
trained chef, his wife, Cindy, a nurse. He in-

sists on fresh ingredients and turns in a quality performance each time he puts on his apron. She cares for her customers like they were her patients. The result—well-prepared, good food, nicely presented with sincere hospitality in immaculate but comfortable surroundings. Everything on the menu is worth recommending, but the pork loin chop and chicken-fried steak are particularly memorable. Try the Wolverine, a prime rib sandwich on a hoagie or some occasional Czech specials, such as the Czech reuben or liver dumpling soup (call ahead to Czech on these specials).

Chances R—York
402-362-7755

Very popular. Be prepared to wait in line for Sunday brunch. Lots of brass and paneling provide a pleasant atmosphere. Nothing exotic on menu, but food and service are consistently good. Excellent pastries.

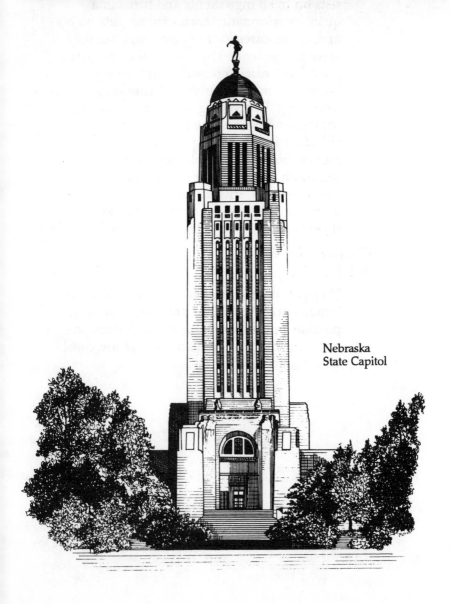

Nebraska
State Capitol

Places that Have Passed Away

Restaurants have a short life expectancy. It may be related to the amount of smoke, sodium, sugar, and cholesterol found on the premises. Perhaps they succumb to too much hard living and too little time. Funny though, you'd think they'd live a long time (doesn't running a restaurant have something to do with fitness?). But grouchy servers, scant promotion, poor location, and tasteless food have killed many a cafe.

> . . . some places were out of business by the time I arrived to check them out.

One of the major problems encountered in researching this book was that some places were out of business by the time I arrived to check them out. And the Lyons Bakery and Cafe in Lyons went out of business after I had visited it three times.

Roadfood and *Goodfood* by Jane and Michael Stern are recognized as gospel on offbeat eating establishments in America. As recently as 1986, the M and M Cafe and Bakery in O'Neill was listed in *Roadfood* as one of the five recommended Nebraska cafes. Here's a taste of what *Roadfood* had to say about the M and M: "We especially favor the sour cream raisin or apricot pies; but there are also cherry, blueberry, apple, peach, coconut, chocolate . . . you get the idea. An oasis on Highway 275."

On reading this account I was, of course, anxious to try it out. After driving an extra fifty miles to make it in time for lunch, you can imagine my disappointment at finding the lights out, the door locked, chairs piled on top of dusty tables, and a For Sale sign in the window. The M and M had passed away.

In a 1983 edition of the Alliance Herald, I read about the resurrection of a long-dead cafe in the village of Angora, a tiny speck on the map about twenty miles northeast of Scottsbluff. Here's what the reporter had to say about the Half-Way Cafe: "There are some sounds making a comeback in Angora, sounds that have been missing for close to a decade, such as the sizzle of a burger on a grill, the clinking of coffee cups, and the laughter of people. And the noise is flowing out of the Half-Way Cafe, a little eatery that's been brought back to life by Purley and Leona Simpson, a pair of upstate New Yorkers who just wanted to try their luck in the restaurant world."

I drove to Angora from Scottsbluff on a hot July day, eager to meet Purley and Leona and find out how a couple from the crowded East could find happiness flipping hamburgers for truckers in Angora, Nebraska. Tumbleweeds piled at the door of the dirty stucco building were the first sign that I would not be interviewing Purley and Leona. Not only was the Half-Way Cafe dead, the whole town was dead. No mystery here about why the cafe died: there were no customers. In fact, the mystery is why the two New Yorkers thought they could make a go of the Half-Way Cafe out here half-way from no where. The only thing moving in Angora that day was a skinny, white dog with brown ears that trotted toward me, confused as to whether he should bark or wag his tail in greeting. I approached the abandoned storefront to see for myself if it was closed for good. The door was locked, the lights were out. I peered in the window. Salt shakers and cups littered the tables. There were no sounds of sizzle, no clinking of cups, no laughter; death

> No mystery here about why the cafe died: there were no customers.

hung in the air. The Half-Way Cafe had passed away—
all the way away, again.

Several years ago a unique restaurant/art gallery was
established in an old building near the railroad tracks
in Fremont. It was called the Brunswick Gallery and
Restaurant. But by the time I got there, it had closed. I
never discoverd whether it was the art or the food that
was bad. When I told an artist friend, Lanny
Fiegenschuh, about this unique restaurant idea, he
described his version of a restaurant/art gallery guaranteed for an early grave: the art would be the low-
quality stuff. There would be plaster black panthers to
set on your TV, lava lamps, and life-size velvet paintings of Elvis. Lanny's name for the place—the Kitsch
Inn.

Restaurant failures also occur close to home, sometimes for obvious reasons. Simple Pleasures, one of my
favorite eating spots in Lincoln, served fine continental
cuisine. But one day it too closed its doors. Unlike the
M and M and the Half-Way Cafes, it had a location on
a busy street corner, but some actually blamed its death
on this busy location—it gave patrons an unobstructed
street-level view of traffic turning left on O Street.
There may be something to that, but I fault the name of
the building itself. After all, would you want to eat in a
place known as the Terminal Building?

(Moral: Please call ahead to make sure an establishment is still alive and to be sure they'll be open
when you arrive.)

123 North 13th, 402-435-9181

Ever dream of being on stage, treading the boards where theatre legends have walked? At Barrymore's Lounge in Lincoln you don't have to dream about it—you are on stage, the stage of the once-famous Stuart Theatre.

The entry door to the lounge is the original stage-door entrance. It's the same door used by Helen Hayes and Mickey Rooney in the heyday of the Stuart Theatre. The light board/control panel to your left is the original, complete with all the equipment. The long ropes on the right as you enter the bar area control all the battens and backdrops now hoisted high over your head. Look up. The vast open area extends 110 feet, that's more than ten stories to the ceiling. The lounge it-self is located right on the stage.

The stars' dressing rooms on the west side of the second floor are now the restrooms. They're all original except for carpet and paint. The chorus's dressing rooms on the second and third floors at the east end are now used for meeting rooms.

Musicians entered the orchestra pit in the base-ment directly below your seats. The individual lights over each table, which create an intimate atmosphere, were created from the footlights at the edge of the pit. The conductor's podium is now used for hors d'oeuvres.

Although space allows only a very small kitchen, the sandwiches are excellent. They are appropriately named the Bogart, Groucho, Garbo, and all, and there's a low-cal one named after the owner, Jim Haberlan, who is on a perpetual diet. I chose the Mickey Rooney, a tasty combination of hot pastrami and turkey on rye with a side of pasta salad.

A unique item on the menu is historic Lebsack's Chili. This dish closely resembles the tasty but grease-laden chili served by the Lebsack Brothers about a block from the present-day Barrymore's. If you were around Lincoln in the 50s and 60s, you'll remember it.

Barrymore's was opened in 1974 by Jim Haberlan, a Lincoln architect with a theatrical bent and a commitment to historic preservation. He has created a one-of-a-kind place to have a drink, enjoy quiet conversation, or simply sit back and listen to some of the best bar music around (from jazz to classical). With an atmosphere like that, it's easy to dream of being a star.

The Bistro—Lincoln

126 North 14th, 402-475-0414

F rom its new quarters on 14th Street in Lincoln, the Bistro has jumped back into the culinary scene. While the menu appears to be the same, the atmosphere has taken a leap into the unknown with a funky Euro-style-loft decor. One carryover from the old location is the elaborate and hugely ornate back bar which anchors the entryway and creates a small saloon in front of a familiar exposed brick backdrop. Still present, too, is the Bistro hallmark: a large vase of gladioli on the bar.

The cafe's dominant colors are now white, gray, and black creating an earnest, trendy look that will appeal to some tastes. But the charm of intimate space, warm brick walls, and the skylight full of green plants—details that helped make the Bistro a favorite destination for years—is now missing.

The Bistro's kitchen and service went through a rocky transition in the move to its present location. I was afraid for a while that the Bistro had been Bistroyed, but the food and service are now approaching their former top-performance levels. For lunch they offer exotic soups (artichoke, lentil, broccoli, etc.) and an array of interesting salad combinations. My favorite is still the Chinese chicken salad, marinated and sauteed chunks of chicken on a bed of greens with a distinctive ginger dressing. The dinner menu includes such items as chicken dijonaise, beef bourguignon, fettuccini bolognese, and duck with cranberry sauce.

The Bistro is regaining momentum. I'm confident the kitchen is on track toward creating the distinctive offerings of the past. Perhaps some of my concern was sentimental attachment to the old location. Now that I've made the adjustment to the new spot, I once again feel it is one of the best restaurants in Lincoln.

The Cookie Company—Lincoln

138 North 12th, 402-475-0625

Don't do it. Don't dare to do it. Don't walk down 12th Street between O and P in Lincoln. You'll encounter a powerful, enticing fragrance there that will lead you, pull you, drag you toward a decadent place known as the Cookie Company. The smell of baking cookies is irresistible—and the Cookie Company knows it. Every time that aroma jerks me inside the door, I accuse owner Elizabeth Wanamaker of treachery in the lowest form. Not content to let the smell gradually escape the premises, she's placed a fan near the ovens which blows the seductive odor out the front door—an invisible salesman sent to hustle the unwary passersby. On days when the temperature gets over 60 degrees, Elizabeth props open the front door; that's chemical warfare!

On football Saturdays she pulls her dirtiest trick of all—cookie hooking. Her helpers pass out free samples in front of the store. Thousands of Cornhusker fans drive home after the game unaware that they've been hooked for life on Cookie Company cookies.

I was hooked long ago, and now come back again and again. The first thing you notice when you enter the narrow shop is a massive array of fresh-baked cookies. These are large cookies, about six inches in diameter. There are at least twenty different varieties, including oatmeal raisin, peanut butter, chocolate chip, banana nut, and my nomination for the world's greatest cookie—macadamia nut. The sight of the cookies drains me of any remaining sales resistance. I usually buy two, sometimes three.

These are Nebraska's best cookies. At only fifty cents apiece, they're a bargain. So be careful where you walk in Lincoln. If you're daydreaming, and wander onto 12th Street, don't say I didn't warn you.

Imperial Palace—Lincoln

707 North 27th, 402-474-2688

Stanley Jou, the owner of the Imperial Palace, says he knows the names of 1500 customers. The last time Katherine and I were there he was able to tell us (correctly) the number of years we'd been regular customers. During that period of time, we've had attentive service, excellent meals, and the delight of being personally greeted by our first names every time we enter the establishment.

This smooth operation is a marvel, and it could be a lesson to other restaurateurs. Staff turnover seems minimal and, no matter who serves the meal, friendly, cheerful, and skillful help is at hand.

The interior evokes Chinese themes. The colorful dining room is tasteful and appropriate to the cuisine; red, black lacquer, and gold trim predominate. Diners will find the atmosphere informal and family-oriented and sometimes a little noisy in the crowded dining room. But the bustle seems comfortable.

The service is extraordinary. It has a subtle rhythm of personal attention; Stanley greets you by name at the door, the hostess shows you to your table, a busboy promptly fills your water glasses, the smiling waiter or waitress fills your tea cups and takes your orders, and the kitchen responds with class and alacrity.

As in most Chinese restaurants, they have a *War and Peace*-length menu. I've read the Palace's several times so I usually start with a large bowl of hot and sour soup and sometimes add appetizers such as crab rangoon or a spring roll. Crab rangoon is a tasty cream cheese, crab, and onion mixture in a deep-fried wonton wrapper. The spring roll is a typical egg roll, also deep-fried. Neither are greasy or oily in taste or texture.

To his regular customers, particularly Asian students, Stanley also serves authentic Chinese dishes, not listed on the menu. An interpreter is recommended, however, for this eating odyssey.

Our favorite entree is mu shu pork, shredded pork with bean sprouts and other Chinese vegetables topped with a wonderful plum sauce and wrapped in a Chinese pancake (think of a thin tortilla or an egg roll wrapper). The flavor is exotic with the plum sauce adding a tangy sweet taste. There's usually more than enough for two people in the order.

The sister Imperial Palace in Omaha is fancier, but just as good. At the Imperial Palace you're treated like royalty, without paying royal prices.

King's Drive In—Lincoln

1650 Cornhusker Hwy., 402-435-8396

Bring back the fifties with posters of Jimmy Dean, Alfred Hitchcock, and Humphrey Bogart. Bring back rock-and-roll with Elvis, the Supremes, Chubby Checker, and the Big Bopper. Bring back the "World's Best Hamburger," mountains of onion rings, and milk shakes served in huge stainless steel containers. King's Drive In has brought all of this back to one of its original locations on Cornhusker Highway.

On the Saturday night I first stopped in, the revived King's was full, and people were waiting to be seated. I went early the next night and barely beat the crowd; when I left, they were lined up again. Surprisingly, the crowd wasn't limited to now-aging boppers trying to relive the past; customers of all ages seem to enjoy this reincarnation of the King's Drive Ins.

Most things in the new King's are about the same. The walls are turquoise, the linoleum black and white checkerboard, the booths orange naugahyde, and the walls sport huge posters of movie stars from the 50s. There is also continuous rock-and-roll music. Missing are the phones at each booth for calling in your order; courteous young servers have replaced them.

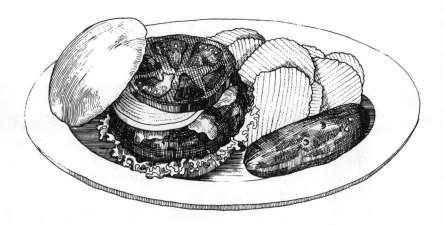

The menu and the taste of the food successfully duplicates the original King's diner-style formula. I ordered the "World's Best Hamburger," fried the old-fashioned way with lots of the familiar pepper flavor. It tasted even better than it did thirty years ago (but then most of us think that the best hamburgers were those served at the hamburger stands of our youth).

The "World's Best" is simple: no exotic seeds cling-
ing to the buns, no lavish red sauce dumped on top of
the meat to camouflage its flavor, no vestigial bun
within a bun, no showy over-thickness of meat—the
downfalls of modern-day artificials. The "World's Best"
is just pure burger. If you want to doctor it up, you can
do that too. It comes with lettuce, tomato, a paper cup
of fresh chopped onions, and another filled with the
mildly seasoned french dressing I remember so well. Of
course, there are french fries and the familiar onion
rings, crisp and not too greasy. The milk shakes come in
metal containers that hold twice as much shake as
McDonald's.

King's is a convertible ride back to the 50s. It's a
ride you'll want to take again. The Big Bopper said it
best, "You knows what I like."

Lee's Restaurant—Lincoln

1940 West Van Dorn, 402-477-4339

Don't think about going to Lee's if you want a quiet,
romantic dinner for two. For before there was
ShowBiz Pizza, there was Lee's Restaurant! The
original Lee's near Pioneer's Park (there's a new one in
East Lincoln) is one of the few restaurants where your
kids can act just like they do at home. And best of all,
the kids' noise isn't traceable to your table; it will simply blend in with the organ music designed to put you
in the mood to go roller-skating. Plus, you can be assured that there will be at least one hundred other kids
there, racing around, yelling, and laughing just as loud

as yours. After you've ordered, relax and have a beer. Being at Lee's before your food is served is like sitting in a sidewalk cafe during the running of the bulls in Pamplona. Lee's is one of the few places where most of the young patrons sweat while they eat.

The atmosphere of Lee's has all the charm of a grade school auditorium. Its decor is unremarkable: wooden booths, formica-covered tables, metal chairs, linoleum floors, and low ceilings. Its function is to withstand child abuse and above all, not to detract from the reason most people come to Lee's—to consume fried chicken. In fact, the only real atmosphere in Lee's is the smell of fried chicken that greets you as you enter the door and step immediately into the ubiquitous waiting line.

Forget about the other entrees on the menu. Stick with the fried chicken. Going to Lee's and ordering anything but chicken is like walking down Broadway and deciding to go to a movie instead of a play. By packing the place since 1945, Lincolnites have proven again and again, that Lee's serves the best fried chicken in town. The chicken is tender and fried in fresh peanut oil, its corn-flake crust extra thick with lots of crunch to the bite.

Along with the chicken they feature heaps of onion rings, a simple lettuce salad accompanied by the familiar three-tub salad dressing server, an aluminum-wrapped baked potato, and a pretty average basket of store-bought rolls.

The finishing touch is that the kids get lollipops, bubble gum, and balloons as you pay your bill. (You can also get some if you hold your hand out and beg. After all, why should the kids get all the goodies? You just paid the bill.)

By the time you walk out, the kids' mouths are full of these sweets. By the time you get to the car, they're either still sucking on the pops or simply tuckered out from all the food and exercise. On the peaceful drive home you and spouse will agree that Lee's is a great way to fill up and quiet down the little ones and thus assure yourselves of a quiet, romantic ride back home.

Misty's—Lincoln

6235 Havelock, 402-466-8424

Misty's offers exactly the atmosphere you'd find in the long hallway leading to your high-school locker room. There are display cases filled with trophies, autographed footballs, and battle-scarred helmets. There is a life-sized quarterback poised to pass in the direction of the cashier and a football-shaped bar. It's an inspiring shrine for football wanna-bees or once-weres. When the place was designed, it's obvious no one consulted a professional decorator. A football coach, no doubt an offensive coordinator, said, "How about spiffin' this place up a bit? Use your imagination. Put some razzle dazzle into it. Wallpaper the john using play diagrams; the X's and O's will create interest."

As you walk past the relics of football warriors, a true football fan can hear the crashing of shoulder pads, see the collision of the middle linebacker with the fullback, and almost smell the sweat. The perfume of grilling steaks fortunately masks the sweat and brings you back to the business at hand—the need to tie into some top-ranked Nebraska beef.

No, don't expect quiche or cobb salad on the menu at Misty's. Don't expect the romance of a strolling musician. This is a strictly macho hangout. At Misty's it's football and beef. The blue-chip star is the prime rib, thick, tender, full of corn-fed flavor, and served in a light brown puddle of its own juice. For triple-threat taste, try the sizzling sirloin steak. It's thick, oozing with its natural juice, pink to slightly red, a real hunk of flavor.

When you walk out of Misty's, you will have the same satisfied feeling of Cornhusker fans after another Big Red victory.

The Oven—Lincoln

201 North 8th, 402-475-6118

See the review of The Indian Oven in Omaha for more information.

The Rotisserie—Lincoln

11th and O Sts., 402-475-9475

M y favorite restaurant in Lincoln is the Rotisserie, and it seems to get better with each visit. After a slow start, this newly redecorated restaurant has finally hit its stride. It manages to stay one step ahead of the pack with attentive service, sophisticated atmosphere, and a menu that is one of the most varied in Lincoln.

In the Grotto, a casual cafe in its lower level, a new but quite familiar face provides a model for graciousness and customer service. The Rotisserie has managed to snag one of the city's most capable restaurateurs, Herb Thomas, formerly of the Lincoln Exchange and Billy's. Herb manages the cellar with polish and elegance. He has a remarkable ability to remember names, faces, and favorite meals, and is a valuable asset to an already outstanding restaurant.

The soups and salads are innovative, and the entrees run the gamut from pasta, duck, chicken and seafood. For light dining I prefer the unusual pizza-like combinations (for example blue cheese and walnut toppings) served on pita bread. Of course, they have a dessert tray filled with goodies that will make you feel guilty, but unrepentant.

The atmosphere is New York—a mix of art-deco and post-modern decor. Every wall is a different color—lavender, peach, purple, and red. The colors are bright, colors you couldn't live with, but which are festive for a night out. Huge oil paintings of plump, exotic women accent the walls. There's also a wonderful painting of a stout couple dancing. Sound different and intriguing? That's the best way to describe the Rotisserie.

Runza Drive Inns

P *erestroika* has come to the state's food industry: when a delegation of Russians visited Nebraska, they sampled a runza, a food that Nebraskans have relished for more than four decades. Their reaction was the same as most Nebraskans—they loved them. As a result runzas will soon be sold in the Soviet Union.

It's not surprising that Russians love runzas. After all, the runza recipe came from Germans who emigrated to Russia before coming to this country. A runza is a mixture of ground beef, cabbage, onions and spices in a loglike loaf of homemade-style dough. The taste is uncommon, but addictive. It's like eating a fragrant, warm Thanksgiving dinner roll filled with a spiced hamburger blend.

The commercial runza is the creation of Sally Everett of Lincoln, using the recipe her mother used on her farm near Sutton. Sally, brother Alex Brening, and brother-in-law Milan Everett opened the first Runza Drive Inn in 1949. It was located in an old corndog stand that Sally bought and moved to a cornfield on the road to Pioneer's Park. In fact, the original Drive Inn still operates at that location. In 1966 Sally's son Don opened his first Runza Drive Inn in Lincoln. By 1979 there were nine outlets, and there are now close to fifty in Nebraska, Colorado, Iowa, and Kansas. Obviously, midwesterners share the German and Russian taste for runzas.

The shops are extremely well managed, and the food and service consistently good. Although the runza is the highlight, I would also recommend the hamburgers and soups. The hamburgers have been voted the best in Lincoln for several years. Katherine's favorite is the ranch burger— lettuce, tomato, and ranch dressing.

If the Russians had discovered the pleasures of a hot runza a lot sooner, the Cold War might have ended long ago.

The Steak House—Lincoln

3441 Adams St., 402-466-2472

T he Hunting Lodge might be a better name for this long-time Lincoln restaurant. Given its tacky Cornhusker Highway location, the Steak House goes to some length to create a far-away atmosphere. In the main dining room, mounted hunting trophies and north-woods artifacts create a rustic atmosphere. The room is quite dark with wagon-wheel chandeliers, a huge fireplace, and stone walls. It's a classic woodsman's fantasy.

Diners eat at tables crowded together with little room to pass between. Checkered cloths and candles grace each table, and the pervasive aroma of grilling meat whets the appetite. The menu tends to be stand-ard steakhouse, not fancy, yet not plain, good food at moderate prices in an atmosphere a cut above the typi-cal Nebraska steakhouse.

The restaurant has been enlarged to include a lounge in the southern half of the building. Known as the Stoney Inn, this warm, inviting bar would be ideal for watching televised football games or celebrating a gridiron victory. Food is also available in the lounge.

For forty years, The Steak House has been a Lincoln tradition because of its consistent quality and rustic atmosphere. It's great casual dining, a perfect spot for a gang of carnivores after a game.

Valentino's—Lincoln

Located in larger Nebraska cities

The three Nebraska football players—whose combined weights might total 755 pounds—had done something they rarely do: skipped lunch, while taking a final exam. Now it was 5 p.m. and they were famished. Where to go to satisfy this gnawing hunger? The answer was obvious and unanimous: Valentino's.

They ordered the all-you-can-eat salad bar and buffet, a tremendous bargain at $5.95 even for normal eaters. But these fellows, whose food consumption is measured in tons, not pounds, could go through $5.95 worth of food at the salad bar alone!

The Valentino's buffet is an Italian cornucopia. After a salad bar that consists of lettuce and spinach salad, fresh vegetables, and loads of cold pasta salads, the Huskers rushed the heavyweight table loaded with trays of pizza of every description. Val's pizza is exquisite, its crust sweet, as is the rich, superbly seasoned tomato sauce. (The pizza is so good that it's one of the things Lincolnites long for when they leave the state. Every other year Nebraskans living in New York City satisfy this craving by having a food bash to which Val's pizza is shipped by the crateful.) In addition to pizza, the buffet tables offer an artistically arranged and constantly maintained supply of all the other Italian favorites—spaghetti, cavatini, lasagna, etc. There is also a large choice of flavorful sauces, including beer cheese, clam, and spicy-Italian meat.

The Huskers attacked the buffet as aggressively as the Black Shirts defense swarms an opponent's passer. They loaded up, packed it in, loaded up and packed it in again. For the other customers it was a great spectator sport. Helpings devoured ranged from a modest three for a 190-pound wide receiver to eight for Oliver, a gigantic middle guard from one of Nebraska's Swedish communities. (Oliver claimed to weigh only 270, but his line coach always said he was only a Hershey bar away from 300.) He ate so much that night that he stripped two notches in his belt and popped a button on his shirt; even his armpits bulged. An hour and a half later, he was still eating cherry pizza for dessert when the others convinced him that if he didn't quit soon, he wasn't going to look good in his swimming suit.

Valentino's has been feeding hungry Nebraskans for years. Val and Zina Wyler ran the Campus Fruit Market for twelve years before they decided that they probably couldn't compete with the supermarkets. So, they converted the market into a pizza parlor featuring a secret pizza recipe that can compete with any in the world, a recipe that had been in Zina's family for years. The result was instant success. In the early 60s, when the spot across the street from UNL's east campus was the only location, I can remember waiting, gladly waiting for over an hour to get in. Fortunately, Valentino's has now expanded so the waits are short (besides, they sometimes serve free pizza to waiting patrons). There are now four locations in Lincoln alone, and over thirty locations scattered over Nebraska and adjoining states.

For great Italian food, together with friendly, efficient service, attractive Italian decor, immaculate presentation, and a relaxing, family-oriented atmosphere, Valentino's is hard to beat—even if you don't play middle guard.

Significant Others—Lincoln

Billy's—Lincoln
1301 H St.
402-474-0084

Politics, good food, and drink mix well at Billy's. Named after Nebraska's illustrious William Jennings Bryan, Billy's is a favorite hangout for politicos from the nearby Capitol.

In 1986, Billy's opened in the historic Noble-Dawes house, which had been built in 1887. Once a fraternity house, (1898 to 1900, Phi Gamma Delta), the house has had many lives. Now attractively restored with three intimate dining rooms, each is named after a famous Nebraska politician. There is also a bar, the Chautauqua Lounge. The atmosphere is homey, but elegant with a political theme. Political memorabilia from William Jennings

Bryan, Charles Dawes, and George Norris grace the walls.

Nader Farahbod has served as chef since the restaurant opened. His recipes include veal (oscar, vitillone, picatta, zingara), rack of lamb, beef (steak diane, filet mignon, and t-bone), as well as fresh fish and scallops flown in from the coasts three times a week. The food and service are excellent.

You won't have to spend any time in smoke-filled rooms, and you won't have to caucus to decide to cast your vote for Billy's.

Coffee House—Lincoln
1342 P St.
402-477-6611

Laid-back intellectual hangout near city campus of UNL, reminiscent of a 50s Bohemian enclave. Every campus needs one. Good place to relax, read, play chess, or debate the problems of the world. Local art shown monthly. Offers a variety of exotic coffees, including cappucino, and herb teas, veggie sandwiches, soups, and mammoth pastries. Enjoyable alternative to burger burnout. A fun place for dessert after a movie.

E11even—Lincoln
1248 O St.
402-434-4111

A continental restaurant perched atop the National Bank of Commerce at 13th & O. Like Maxine's in Omaha, this is a dress-up spot for people who crave heights. The view from the lounge is the best. Check out E11even.

Hi-Way Diners—Lincoln
(Five locations in Lincoln)

Popular diners scattered around Lincoln. Trucker's helpings. Don't eat all weekend and have the Monday special—homemade biscuits with chicken and gravy that overwhelms the plate and the palate. Eat here and you'll have a heavy foot on the pedal.

Papa John's—Lincoln
114 South 14th St.
402-477-7657

In traveling from one end of the state looking for different eateries, I almost overlooked a good one only a block from where I work. Papa John's is a new Greek restaurant in Lincoln. Counter ordering creates a fast food atmosphere amid mauve and brass decor, scattered Greek posters, and authentic Greek music. You can get American cooking, but go for Greek daily specials. My favorite is Greek-style chicken, very juicy and tender with strong lemon-butter flavor. The Greek potatoes cooked in olive oil and Greek spices are unusual and very good. On Saturdays they serve a delicious combination plate. Desserts are just as good as the entrees. The three I tried—finike (a cinnamon cookie), Greek apple cake; and Golloutobourikio (vanilla custard cake)—were all terrific. It's food well worth the walk.

The Renaissance, Cornhusker Hotel—Lincoln
333 South 13th
402-474-7474

Eating in the Renaissance of the Cornhusker Hotel, you can watch your meal go up in flames. There is some charm to tableside cooking, but at the Renaissance they apply flame to everything; if I hadn't kept my hand on my water glass, they might have poured a slick of brandy on it and torched it too.

All kidding aside, the Renaissance is a classy place with continental food and service equal to the finest big-city restaurants. It has received a four-diamond rating from the American Automobile Association; the food and the elaborate presentation demonstrate that the recognition is well-deserved. The excellent seafood includes scampi, Mahi-Mahi, salmon, and orange roughy. Of course, beef is also served. The dessert tray is dazzling and loaded with chocolate delights. Of course, you can also get your dessert flamed!

Blackstone
Hotel,
Omaha
Home of
Reuben
Sandwich

An Essay

N ebraska is a magnificent state. It has the Sandhills with oceans of prairie grasses and wildflowers; the unsurpassed spectacle of 500,000 Sandhill cranes migrating through the Platte Valley each spring; the Niobrara, a great canoe river and a unique biological crossroads; Fort Robinson and the history-laden area of the Pine Ridge; and many other scenic and cultural attractions. Nebraskans sometimes overlook these natural wonders, though, and direct energy and resources into misguided attempts to attract the tourist dollar. I call these lame, manufactured attractions Tourist Distractions. Here are some that come to mind:

The Gerald R. Ford Birthplace, Omaha. When Omaha decided to pay tribute to President Ford, the house in which he was born was long gone. What to do? You can't exhibit memorabilia in a vacant lot. The problem was solved by building a shrine-like structure and rose garden better suited to Lady Bird Johnson than a president known more for his athletics than aesthetics. A few items—ashtrays, a pipe, and of course, golf clubs—are displayed in a kiosk. Other than that, there's nothing presidential to see except for marble plaques recapping the names of the presidents and their states. If you just drive by and don't get out to read the plaque, you would conclude that President Ford was born in a rose garden. At the very least, they should have installed a putting green.

> Paddle wheelers aren't known for their cuisine, and if you don't like the band, there's no escape.

The Belle of Brownville, Brownville. The Belle is a renovated paddle wheeler that offers trips on the Missouri River. The concept is great, but the major attraction turns out to be a closeup view of the Brownville Nuclear Power Station. Actually you get two good looks, coming and going. Definitely skip the dine 'n dance cruise. Paddle wheelers aren't known for their cuisine, and if you don't like the band, there's no escape.

Elkhorn Valley Rail Car Company, Fremont. This is a twenty-mile train trip from Fremont to Nickerson and back that passes through prime corn country, row upon row upon row of corn. "Look out the windows," the guide shouted above the clickety-clack and engine noise. "As far as you can see is hybrid corn. Can you hear me? THIS...IS...HYBRID...CORN!"

Generally, I don't recommend any eating establishment that moves, but in this case, you probably ought to skip the scenic day trip to Nickerson and try the dinner train from Fremont to Hooper. They serve wine.

World's Largest Covered Wagon, Dahle (an unincorporated village near the Milford exit on I-80). In 1964, Ken Dahle, operator of a service station, had the idea for "something that would stand out on the Interstate." He designed a service station topped with the world's largest covered wagon. No need to stop; you can see it clearly from the road.

Homestead National Monument, Beatrice. Katherine tells the story of a childhood trip to what was then a newly established tourist attraction and the site of the first claim made under the Homestead Act of 1862. Her family expected to see artifacts, hear interpretive discussions by learned Park Service rangers, and stand in the very spot where the claim was staked. What they found was a cinderblock building with a novice ranger who moved uneasily from display to display as they made the grand tour. At that time, it was a pretty meager place, and they felt sorry for the anxious ranger who pulled duty in Beatrice instead of Yosemite.

They walked from one homely little museum case to another, trying to make polite comments to the ranger who followed close at hand. In the very last case they spied a few dull but sturdy-looking frontier dishes. Peering closely at the case, her mother wondered aloud, "What kind of dishes are these?" "Well," replied the young ranger in his most serious interpretive tone, "The one back there's a plate, that one's a cup, and this is a saucer."

In all fairness, I should add that since 1962, the Park Service has turned Homestead National Monument into a tourist attraction of substance. It is now the second largest such center in the National Park Service's ten-state Midwest region, and according to Superintendent Randy Baynes, one of the finest facilities in the nation.

> The ride takes you around a small pond to peer at big brown catfish.

Glass-Bottomed Boat Rides, Fort Kearney Museum, Kearney. When I think of glass-bottom boats, I think of California's Catalina Island or the coral reefs of the Carribbean. The ride at the Fort Kearney Museum (not to be confused with the Fort Kearney State Historical Park) takes you around a small pond to peer at big brown catfish. The day I visited, however, the ride was closed due to algae.

Overlook of Lake McConaughy, near Ogallala. The best view of this tribute to the Corps of Engineers is high on a bluff above the dam. Where there could be picnic tables, a small park, or at the very least, a plaque commemorating the prowess of engineers and earth movers, there stands a plain building. On the landward side is Hilltop Inn, a restaurant with what the *World-Herald* claims is "a spectacular lake view unmatched in Nebraska," but what is mostly an unremarkable view of a parking lot. On the other side, however, over-looking the largest lake in the state with its magnificent vistas for breath-taking sunsets, is the immense picture window of the office of the Corps of Engineers. The way I figure it, the taxpayers provided millions just so those fellows could have a view.

The Baking Company—Omaha

7609 Pacific, 402-397-2447

T en years ago Linda Herzog was sitting around at home on a cold February day watching soap operas and wondering if this was all there was to life. She had dreamed of being creative, of being an artist, a writer, a dancer. But those talents were not hers. What could she do and do well? Then the answer came to her: she could cook creatively and well. With that conclusion came the idea for the creation of a gourmet restaurant, the birth of the Baking Company.

This restaurant falls outside the category of typical Nebraska fare. A cross between a bakery, a coffeehouse, and a white-tablecloth restaurant, it's continental and West-Coast trendy in atmosphere. From the peach-colored walls; oak tables and chairs; black, peach, and green floral upholstery and roman window shades; taupe carpeting, and art on the walls, you know this is the perfect spot for a ladies' lunch. (In fact, my favorite painting in the place is a large, bright acrylic of women dining.) But men enjoy the Baking Company as well. It strictly adheres to the philosophy that in gourmet cooking there can be no shortcuts without compromising quality. Fresh ingredients, attention to detail, and constant variety in the menu are what make the Baking Company memorable.

The breadth of the menu suggests that you could eat there every two weeks and never order the same thing. Now that's variety. Let me dazzle you with a few of the selections available throughout the year: for appetizers there are garlic scallops; caramelized onion tart on puff pastry; chicken chili; and baked cheese with walnuts, brown sugar, and peppercorns. For lunch choose the Sonoma special: turkey, apples, celery, and walnuts served on a melon slice; hot walnut chicken; and the salad sampler (any three salads): tuna, walnut, chicken, almond chicken, egg, Sonoma, cream cheese veggie. For dinner, how about the chicken toscana, smoked Cajun sausage, or angel hair St. Jacques?

Appropriate to its name, the Baking Company serves a basket containing a variety of baked goods—biscuits, coffee cake, and banana bread—with each meal. It's yet another extra touch that makes the place distinctive.

But Linda herself would say that the best thing about the Baking Company is its desserts. The serving procedure is simple: after your meal stroll to the bakery counter and select a dessert. I couldn't decide between the strawberry cream torte, red raspberry muffin, and chocolate mousse, so I decided to turn dessert into grazing time and sampled all three. Like everything else, they were outstanding.

Omaha food critics are universal in their praise of Linda Herzog's innovative offerings. The *Omaha World-Herald* says that her whimsy "is what makes the Baking Company special, creative, usually exciting. Unlike most people with this attitude, Linda Herzog also manages to focus it into a unique, moderately priced, often surprising dining experience."

Omaha is darned lucky that Linda cooks better than she can paint, write, or dance.

Bohemian Cafe—Omaha

1406 South 13th St., 402-342-9838

I n the last half of the nineteenth century, a wave of European immigrants swept into Nebraska. There were Germans, Swedes, Irish, Czechs, and others. At the turn of the century, one out of every five Nebraskans had been born in another country. They settled in pockets around the state—the Germans in Grand Island and Norfolk, the Swedes in Stromsburg and Oakland, and Czechs in Wilber and Clarkson. And Omaha got a little bit of everything. Thus, Nebraska became not only a melting pot (or perhaps an Irish Stew) of nationalities, but its immigrants introduced a mix of wonderful ethnic dishes and cafes. One of the best known of these eateries, the Bohemian Cafe, has thrived in the old world atmosphere of south Omaha.

The radio jingle for the Bohemian Cafe goes, "It's dumplings and kraut today at the Bohemian Cafe." But they serve much more than just dumplings and kraut. They have a full line of thigh-expanding Czech meals, including boiled beef in dill gravy, spicy sweet-and-sour cabbage, roast duck, and my favorite, a homely but delicious soup called liver dumpling.

Decor is austere; there are a few Czech greetings painted on the walls and a collection of Jim Beam bottles, but everyone is too busy enjoying the plentiful Czech specialties to notice. The fare is simple, but good, and the bill never stings. Czech it out.

Butsy LeDoux's—Omaha

1020 Howard, 402-346-5100

B utsy LeDoux was a famous Cajun chef from the bayou country of Louisiana. The restaurant that bears her name serves food for the culinary adventurer. Butsy is gutsy. Forget about steak, chicken, and spaghetti. Here's a restaurant that promises to take your taste buds into unexplored territory.

Throw away your inhibitions. Order boiled crayfish flown in daily and cooked in a peppery bouillon. Tie a bib around your neck, break the slimy critter in two, suck the juices out of the head, and then peel and eat the tail...delicious! Ready for more adventure? Mount up with some angels on horseback—grilled oysters wrapped in bacon served on toast points; jump into some jambalaya—a rice dish with tomatoes, onions, pepper, chicken, ham, sausage and shrimp; do the voodoo stew—it's a bewitching blend of beef, okra, tomatoes, onions, spinach, red beans, and special seasonings.

Like most Cajun restaurants, some items on the menu are "blackened" or burned. That's where I draw the line. I've eaten too many hotdogs my kids dropped in the campfire to order burned food on my night out. I'd rather sink my teeth into cubed alligator. (They serve that too.)

If you're downright timid, order muffuletta, a New Orleans hoagie with olive-giardiniera dressing. They also have shrimp creole, barbecued chicken, and the Southern version of one of Nebraska's favorite dishes—chicken-fried steak.

Whether you're adventurous or timid, Butsy LeDoux's cooking is the next best thing to eating in the French Quarter. As they say in Cajun country: "I guar-onn-tee it."

Cafe de Paris—Omaha

1228 South 6th, 402-344-0227

I t costs at least $600 to fly to Paris for dinner. If you want to save your money, the closest thing to dinner in a small Parisian cafe is a trip to Omaha's Cafe de Paris.

The Cafe de Paris is Nebraska's entry into the culinary stratosphere. Elegant, gracious, attentive service abounds. The food is, of course, French and laden with the basics of classic French cuisine—butter, cream, and fine wine.

Located in an unlikely looking small house, the cafe is tucked away in a semi-residential area on the south side of downtown. The unremarkable exterior offers no clue to the treasures inside. This restaurant recreates an era when dining was an art. Waiters hover, the linens are immaculate, and patrons feel as though they've just joined a very exclusive and very elegant private club. I felt like I should have signed up for a refresher course in table manners.

Katherine and I were celebrating a special event with friends (anniversaries and birthdays) when we dined at the Cafe de Paris. The food and wine were equal to the occasion. My entree was a steak of poached salmon with melted butter and an exquisite sauce. Each mouthful brought a marvelous shock of pleasure that plain-food Nebraskans seldom experience.

This is Nebraska's top spot for the grand splurge, the perfect place to celebrate a really special occasion. But I warn you, it's expensive. Go once after each inheritance or when you win the lottery. Also, it's no place to go for a diet meal; the entrees are 1000 calories a sniff, and if you finish off a perfect evening with one of their decadent desserts, you should feel guilty for a week. Not to worry. Just look at your bill and figure the calories-per-dollar ratio. At these prices, you want to get your money's worth.

Cardinal Bar and Cafe—Omaha

4820 South 24th, 402-733-6882

I 've met lots of cooks in my travels across Nebraska. After all this practice, I think I can spot a great cook when I see one. When I met Marta Kovalskas, I knew instantly that she was a great cook. Perhaps it was her warm smile, the way she wore her apron, or her ability to describe an enormous list of her favorite dishes. But most important, it was her zest, an un-bridled enthusiasm for good food and gracious hospitality.

Marta is Lithuanian and her cooking could be described as the kind of food necessary to keep one hard at work in the fields or factories of her homeland. Another of her specialities is Jewish cooking for as a teenager she learned this cuisine from the grandmother

in a Jewish household. Given a day's advance notice, Marta will prepared all kinds of eastern European fare. In her vast repertoire is gefilte fish (chopped fish in a very strong horseradish sauce, guaranteed to clear your sinuses), herring with mush-rooms and tomatoes, veal birds, stuffed cabbage, sweet and sour cabbage, veal pock-ets, Russian potato kugel (something like a quiche), and potato pancakes with sour cream or applesauce.

What she likes most is to serve a group in the eve-ning after her regular patrons have gone. Call ahead and order whatever you want. She can fix it. She serves as cook, waitress and entertainment. Ask her about her recipes, her background and her philosophy, and she'll keep you entertained for hours. A marvelous storyteller, she relates how a portly gentlemen came dressed in a business suit. He sat down and asked her, "Where's the sweet stuff?" "I say, not for you," she recounts wagging her finger as if scolding. "The next day I find out he's a judge."

She hovers eager for comments on the meal and ready to explain each individual ingredient. "Did you like that? Was this too hot for you? I put a lot of spice in that dish. It'll keep you peppy."

If you just drop in, her regular fare is also very good. I've had the pork-filled dumplings swimming in delicious gravy, spicy sauerkraut, barbecued feather bones, roast duck, and an outstanding oxtail soup. Lunches average only about $4.50, dinner is about $5.50 and the reservation dinners run about $10.

The Cardinal Bar and Cafe is really two places in one. The bar is in the front of the building, a former branch of Commercial Federal. It's a typical working-man's bar. The back dining room is "Marta's Picnic." It's nothing fancy; the decor is old wood paneling, beer signs, an odd lot of tables and booths, and a couple of pictures of old South Omaha. It is here in the midst of neighborhood characters that Marta works her culinary magic and serves it on styrofoam plates ("The kitchen's too small for a dishwasher.")

I almost missed the Cardinal. I'm glad I didn't. It's one of those gems that supper scouts dream about.

9405 North 48th, 402-571-2609

Del Jones is daring. He does things most of us wouldn't consider. He started a company, D & D Salads, and proved that an item considered to be highly perishable could be shipped in trucks to forty-one states. Last year his company sold $20 million worth of trucked-in, pre-packaged salad.

It figures that someone with that kind of marketing genius could certainly carve out another niche for himself. Two years ago he started a "fine-dining barbecue restaurant." Now if that isn't a contradiction in terms. Fine dining and barbecue don't mix; I suppose because it's much more embarrassing to drop a big glob of sauce on a nice tie or silk blouse than on a Big Red sweatshirt which quickly soaks it up. Del has elevated eating barbecue to a fine art. No slabs of dripping ribs on waxed paper with white bread on the side; his ribs are served on pewter plates with pewter goblets and utensils. No stack of paper napkins to keep the sauce off your face; Del provides warm, moist hand towels. And the Rack isn't a battered shack with drooping window curtains and rickety chairs and wobbly tables. The huge, pine log cabin looks like a mountain ski lodge with a fireplace at one end and pine greenery scattered about. Yes, Del has violated the rule that guides any good barbecue buff —the dumpier the place, the better the "Q."

Of course, Del's barbecue is different, too. He conducted a taste test with his own employees to arrive at a "secret sauce." Although the reddish-brown color reminds of the typical southern-style sauce, the taste is sweet, mild, and vinegary, a far cry from the downhome variety I've grown to love. Like his country colleagues, however, he does cook his meat slowly over oak or hickory to get the smoked flavor. His offerings

include two kinds of ribs, chicken, ham, and brisket, all
served sauceless so the purists can taste the smoke
flavor before ladeling the sauce out of the warm pewter
pitcher provided on the side.

D & D's Rib Rack, like Del Jones, is a different
breed. It's pleasant and should be successful. It's not
the best barbecue you'll ever eat, but in a state where
barbecue is about as scarce as trees in the Sandhills,
you have to relax your "Q" standards just a little. Besides, it's the best barbecue you'll ever eat in a log cabin
on a pewter plate.

Empanada House—Omaha

4109 L St., 402-731-7369

Arby's, Burger King, Rax, McDonalds, Hardy's, fast
food—novocaine for the American palate—fast,
flat, and forgettable. Fast food is simply a fuel stop—a
place to buy lunch much the same way a motorist buys
gasoline; a place to eat rather than dine.

L Street in Omaha is fast food alley. Bright signs
lure diners into crowded asphalt parking lots. We rush
inside to stand in line, read the plastic menu on the
wall overhead, then watch while our order is punched
into a computer. Our burgers, made from pre-shaped,
pre-weighed frozen patties, have the chewiness of
styrofoam and all the flavor of raw eggplant—that is, if
you can distinguish any flavor after the meat has been
slapped between two slabs of cardboard and disguised
under a heap of lettuce, tomato, pickle, mustard, catsup, and "special sauce." The wrapped or boxed
sandwich is artistically presented on a sheet of paper

covering a plastic tray (no plate, plastic or otherwise). Isn't this an efficient way to eat?

As I drove by yet another fast food outlet, an inner voice suggested: "Slow down. Go on a fast food fast." And that's exactly what I did. I slowed down to discover one of L Streets best-kept secrets.

At 41st and L streets, a hand-painted sign on a small brick building (no neon) said simply: Empanada House, parking in the rear. I parked in one of the five stalls in the rear and sat down at one of the five tables. The room was decorated with a South American motif—pastel pink walls, abstract paintings, simple crafts, and photographs of Chilean scenes. In the quiet, relaxed atmosphere a delectable aroma filled the air, and the fast-food world outside seemed far away.

I was greeted by Joaquin and Fulvia Lieva who operate the Empanada House, the only Chilean restaurant in the Midwest. If the cooking done by Fulvia is typical Chilean fare, it's surprising that the Empanada House is the only one around. Unlike a lot of Mexican dishes which seem overly seasoned and smothered with heavy cheese sauce, Chilean-style food is delicately seasoned with only a moderate use of sauce. The dishes were very mild. Yet on each table was a small pot of fiery salsa, guaranteed to burn a hole in your tongue.

I ordered the empanada after Joaquin explained it is the most typical Chilean dish. Empanadas are meat, seafood, or cheese turnovers, shaped like small submarines. The sandwich was wrapped in home-baked dough—smooth, shiny, and lightly browned—and filled with chopped beef flavored with onions, olives, raisins, and eggs. It tasted a little like a runza, but with thicker dough and a variety of ingredients. An appetizer version of the empanada is lightly fried and filled with cheese, spinach or chicken.

Another excellent choice is pastel de choclo, which in my fractured Spanish means a light-colored chocolate dish. I had clearly missed the mark. In this spectacular item, the bottom of a clay container is covered with sauteed chopped beef, onions, raisins, and spices. The next layer of boned chicken is covered by a thick corn souffle. The layered concoction is baked in the oven until it is a golden brown. Delicious.

The Chilean version of an American hot dog, completos, is a foot-long doused with sauerkraut, tomatoes, onions, homemade mayonnaise, and mustard served on a hoagie bun. I think I'll pick up a sack of them the next time I go to the College World Series.

There are several delicious desserts. My favorite was the sopaipillas chilena which bears no resemblance to the Mexican variety. These are made from a sugar cookie dough of squash, flour, and milk and are served in a warm sauce of orange juice and brown sugar. Magnificent!

Even the drinks are exotic. Try the jugo en agua, a delightful blend of melon, peaches, grapes and water.

After the meal, I was contented and relaxed. I had made new friends, enjoyed wonderful new cuisine, and been reminded once again of the difference between eating and dining.

The French Cafe—Omaha

1017 Howard, 402-341-3547

F or twenty years, Omaha's French Cafe in the Old Market has been a hallmark of elegance and sophistication. Years after my last visit, I dined there again, only to discover to my pleasure that the more things change, the more they remain the same.

Just off the bar is an impressive room for a pre-meal drink. Step down into what could be a drawing room in a chateau in the Loire Valley. There is a high ceiling, and the walls are adorned with massive stags' heads and museum-size oil paintings. A huge, ornate fireplace dominates one corner. The eighteenth-century decor is an interesting contrast to the mood of the main dining room. The chocolate-brown interior is murky and dark with twinkling votive candles mounted in odd corners on the long wall, as though stars were shining in the horizon. Each table has its own small lamp suspended from the high ceiling. The mood is intimate and warm, an atmosphere unlike any other. The atmosphere evokes France. Huge black-and-white photos of French citizens at market, French antiques, and an enormous candelabrum create a continental ambiance.

The menu is not completely French, but inventive and contemporary, and features formal dinners as well as lighter, less expensive bistro fare. Katherine and I had an excellent caesar salad, an unusual soup, and a light entree. As always, this was a meal to celebrate; and we toasted two decades of success for the French Cafe.

Garden Cafe—Omaha

One Pacific Place, 402-397-1991

S omething different is going on at the Garden Cafe in Omaha. Look around. The bright windows and cheery green-and-white interior feel as good as a first cup of coffee in the morning. Freshly baked rolls, muffins, and desserts entice customers at the bakery case. The bustling, informal atmosphere of content-looking blue-collar workers and business people could be a deli in Aspen or Santa Fe.

The menu is encyclopedic, a huge list in fine print. There are twenty omelettes, multiple pancakes and waffles, eleven types of "custom eggs"—chicken benedict, sombrero eggs (scrambled eggs, potatoes, chili, cheese, tomato, onions, sour cream, salsa, "hot and gooey" and served in a tortilla shell with fresh fruit and a muffin), and twelve kinds of potato casseroles. The cooks must have computers to remember all those dishes. Don't forget the orange juice— freshly squeezed, pulpy, and eminently sippable, like a fine wine. And what about some french-dipped raisin bread—a french toast dotted with raisins, crisp and golden brown on the outside, but not soggy on the inside, with a warm pitcher of syrup on the side.

While designed to serve busy working people, the cuisine takes no shortcuts. You can get breakfast any time, but lunch and dinner are equally appealing. The Garden Cafe has three locations in Omaha. I might never eat at home again.

Heaven Scent—Omaha

2418 North 24th, 402-346-9575

T he pleasant voice on the phone purred, "Yes, we stay open until 6 p.m., unless we run out of food" I asked, "Do you have any chitterlings tonight?" "No hon, Monday's chittlin's, but we got things just as good—smothered pork chops, roast chicken and turkey, dressing and gravy, red beans, cabbage, and great cornbread." I asked her to save some of each. "You know I will. Hurry on down now, y'hear."

Two hours later, just before closing time, I walked into Heaven Scent, an authentic soul-food restaurant on Omaha's north side. I met the voice on the phone, Hattie Washington, and one of the owners, Laura Sledge. For the next hour we carried on like old friends. We chatted about food. ("Hattie, what do you put in this dressing?" "Now Richard, you know I can't tell you any of my secrets.") We joked about my ignorance of soul food. ("You've never had sweet potato pie? Why, that's like never having a hot dog!") And we laughed about how much food they piled on my plate ("Laura, I can't eat all that and be able to get up and walk out of here." "Richard, it's almost closing time, and if you don't eat it, it won't get eaten.")

It was like a family reunion with two favorite aunts who like to feed a scrawny-looking nephew. You know the looks they give when you say you're full.

Heaven Scent is described by Dennis Gibson, one of the owners, as a Christian soul-food restaurant. Christian music plays constantly, religious pictures add to the decor, and an atmosphere of sincere Christian love abounds. Laura Sledge sums up Heaven Scent's philosophy: "People come here kind of down sometimes, and we cheer them up. We tell them God loves them and that their troubles will only last a short time. He would put no more on you than you can bear."

I explained that I wanted to sample a little of everything. They ignored my request and gave me a lot of everything in the steam table. It was delicious. The turkey and chicken fell off the bone and were perfectly seasoned. The dressing was spiced with Cajun seasonings, and the cornbread reminded me of my grandmother's cornbread drowned in melted butter, molasses, or sorghum. Even the cabbage and spicy red beans hit the spot.

I got there too late for the house specialty, pork chops smothered in gravy. They were also out of greens—collard, turnip and mustard. The women gently chided me for getting there too late for the chops and greens. I wouldn't have had room for them on my plate anyway.

Hattie invited me to come back for some chitterlings. She said, "Our customers go hog wild over our chittlin's." Speaking of hogs, I did sample pigs' ears for the first and last time.

The next time I visit Heaven Scent I'm going to call ahead to reserve peach cobbler and sweet potato pie. Laura promised it's better than pumpkin pie.

As I walked out, I noticed the sign by the door, "God Bless You, and Come Again." I knew I'd come again. The down-home food was something I'd miss, and I wouldn't want my two new aunts to worry about whether I was getting enough to eat.

The Indian Oven—Omaha

1010 Howard, 402-342-4856

If you want to steal away to a fine ethnic restaurant, some might suggest a trip to the East or West Coast, but Nebraskans have a much shorter trip. We have a hidden treasure within our borders—the Indian Oven, an exotic eatery par excellence!

The Indian Oven is a long-time landmark of Omaha's Old Market district. A tiny storefront, the cafe appears to be the standard, white-washed brick cafe. Inside the narrow dining room, however, the owners have created a warm yet sophisticated atmosphere with Indian tapestries, a few bronze decorative objects, soft ragas playing in the background, and the slightly sweet smell of incense. The lighting is meager, adding charm.

The menu is elaborate. There is the full range of choices from appetizers to entrees to desserts plus full bar service. A special feature is the selection of breads, but they're not your typical variety. All are rather flat and uncommon to the midwest. I recommend trying several. Entrees include chicken, fish, lamb, beef, and vegetarian selections. Portions are ample; half portions are available. Saag meat is a favorite: stewed lamb and spinach in a savory sauce. It has a very plain appearance, looking somewhat like an over-cooked stew, but its flavor is delicious and unlike anything else you may have tasted.

My favorite appetizer is vegetarian samosas, little dough pies lightly fried. Mulligatawny soup is also a good starter, but the taste of cilantro is strong and may not be to everyone's liking. Chicken tikki and chicken korma are good choices for entrees, but they tend to be spicy. Your servers can steer you to entrees that may be more suitable to Western palates. Tandoori shrimp and chicken are popular for that reason. Both have brilliant red coloring because of the way that they are prepared, but neither will offend the sensitive stomach.

You may also want to visit the Indian Oven's sister restaurant, the Oven, in Lincoln's Haymarket district. The menus seem identical, but the surroundings are quite different. The Oven is much more spacious and modern, a wonderful addition to Lincoln, but it feels more like the converted industrial space it is than the quaint, ethnic eatery in Omaha. Katherine and I like both very much, but eat most often in Lincoln because of its proximity and the live music offered once in a while.

For the uninitiated, Indian food may seem forbidding, but by asking the servers about each dish and visiting often, diners will enjoy a wonderful, flavorful adventure.

Johnny's —Omaha

4702 South 27th, 402-731-4774

I n the early spring of 1969 a heifer from the Omaha Stockyards tried to jump out of the fire into the frying pan: She broke out of the nearby yards and tried to bull her way through the front doors of Johnny's Cafe. Even diners who like their steak rare thought that was a bit much.

To my knowledge, Johnny's has never had a more dramatic instance of diners meeting dinner in its sixty-eight year history, but a lot of beef has passed through those doors. Traditionally, Sandhills' ranchers would ship their cattle by train or truck to the Omaha Stockyards; after a day of negotiating in the pens with cattle buyers, the ranchers and their tired ranch hands looked forward to a meal at Johnny's.

The atmosphere in the beef palace known as Johnny's is masculine and opulent. Large cattle murals on the walls, lots of red and gold, huge black wooden arches, brass chandeliers, and oversized high-back chairs make you feel like a cattle baron.

The food also befits royalty. As is the case in all the very best steakhouses of the Midwest, everything at Johnny's is made from scratch. They age and cut their own beef, bake their own bread, and provide many extra touches, such as an appetizer tray of special cottage cheese spread, and baked potatoes that are served without a wrapping of tin foil. Prime rib is their best seller with a variety of cuts ranging from eleven to seventeen ounces. The New York strip is the favorite steak. Heavy hitters can take on a seventeen-ounce T-bone or the twenty-four-ounce porterhouse. If you're concerned about your heart, Johnny's is one of the few restaurants in Omaha to meet the American Heart Association's guidelines for "Happy Heart Cuisine."

Not only is the beef delicious at Johnny's; it's a bargain. After the heifer incident, cafe owner Jack Kawa remembers receiving a call from a San Francisco radio host during which the interviewer asked about Johnny's steak prices. Jack says that when the guy found out how inexpensive the steaks were, he said he was going hop the next plane, because they were about half the price of San Francisco steaks.

Nebraskans don't have to take long trips to eat outstanding beef at "the best of the few remaining stockyard steakhouses in America."

La Strada—Omaha

3125 South 72nd St., 402-397-8389

G oing to a place with linen tablecloths, fresh flowers, candlelight, and soft classical music in the background is enough to overwhelm even those men who think they lack romantic inclinations. I proposed to Katherine at La Strada, and she and I've been going back regularly since.

La Strada is intimate, with modern, sophisticated decor. The atmosphere is classy, yet relaxed and comfortable. The main dining room is done in light colors with brick and blond wood and just the right modern art on the walls. Mirrors in the front create roominess and a skylight in the back opens up the space to the outside. The patio off of the dining room is one of my favorite places when the weather is just right. It is nicely landscaped and filled with red chairs and faux marble tables. Brightly colored Cinzano umbrellas above each table complete the feeling of an Italian piazza.

But it is not only the atmosphere that makes La Strada my favorite Omaha restaurant. The food is always wonderful. Owners, Sebastiano, (Subby) and Sebastiana (Nellie) Floridia emigrated from Sicily, a southern Italian region known for its heavy, spicy tomato sauces. However, when they started the restaurant ten years ago, they imported a chef from the old country. He is primarily responsible for the lighter, more delicate sauces and flavors associated with northern Italian cooking which is featured at La Strada.

The specials change every couple of weeks so there is always something new on the menu that includes fresh seafood, beef, lamb, and chicken. I usually can't resist the veal and pasta dishes which are consistently unique. Portions are ample and the prices reasonable, given the quality. Dinners range from $7 to $30, the lunches from $4 to $7.

The desserts are also special at La Strada. You can boost your calorie count with a selection which looks too rich in the first place and then exceeds your expectations, or you can go for the lighter, homemade gelato (Italian ice cream).

The consistency of the food and the attentive, polished service reflect the efforts of this family operation. Nellie and son Enzo are responsible for the kitchen. Subby, a diminutive but distinguished man who is a barber by day, serves as host in the evenings and daughter, Connie Pera, serves as hostess for lunch.

For a fantastic evening in a restaurant that is in the upper strata, you can't beat La Strada. But don't take your sweetheart there unless you're ready to get married. On the other hand, go ahead. If you're as fortunate as I, you'll have found a great restaurant as well as a great marriage.

Mr. C's Steakhouse—Omaha

5319 North 30th, 402-451-1998

Everyday is Christmas at Mr. C's. Twinkling multi-colored lights are strung everywhere. Thousands and thousands of lights decorate entryways and dining rooms. It all started in 1956 when one of the waitresses asked owners Yano and Mary Caniglia to leave up the Christmas decorations until her husband returned from active duty in Korea. He didn't get back until July. In the meantime, the staff put up more lights. The customers liked the effect, and the lights have been up ever since.

The rest of the decor is remarkable: there is an iridescent mural of Venice on one wall, a backlit 3-D diorama of a Sicilian village on another, and life-sized pictures of a family and customers standing on a veranda. It's unlike anything else you've ever seen. Kids of all ages love it. And yes, strolling violinists complete the Italian atmosphere.

Mr. C's, started in 1953, as a small drive-in, had no plumbing when it was first leased. However, one of the proprietor's first purchases was an electric sign with 4,000 lights that cost $25,000. (Lights have always been a high priority with Mr. C.) Then he built a dining room beside the drive-in. Addition after addition has turned the structure into a huge conglomerate of dining rooms. There's a 225-seat banquet room, and the outdoor Piazza di Maria (named after Mr. C's wife), which opened in 1988, seats 500 diners. Despite its capacity, Mr. C's always seems packed.

The menu features Italian food and steaks, but you can also get chicken, shrimp, and occasional specialities such as stuffed bell peppers. The minestrone soup, which appears on every table every night except Saturday, is a spicy, memorable concoction.

Mr. C himself adds to the year-round holiday atmosphere by greeting his guests personally. He's a jolly man, and dressed in the proper attire, he could pass for Santa Claus. Amid all the Christmas decor, I suspect that Santa Claus would hardly be noticed at Mr. C's.

M's Pub—Omaha

422 South 11th, 402-342-2550

Pubs are usually small, quiet places. Not M's Pub. It seems large and open because of its high ceilings, leftover from its former life as a fruit and vegetable warehouse. And it certainly isn't quiet. Its atmosphere is sophisticated, but bustling. It's a place to talk (you don't have to shout), to laugh, to have a great time. It's filled with interesting people, an upbeat tempo, an electric atmosphere. M's is like a strong cup of coffee or a downhill ski run—exciting.

In fact, M's feels more like an indoor sidewalk cafe than a pub. Its mirrors create light and reflect the patrons from every angle. Customers, usually engaged in animated conversation, perch on barstools around the large green marble bar, made even more distinctive by a vase of flowers and candelabra. Along the wall are high tables with stools providing a ringside view of the passersby. M's also has a real sidewalk cafe when weather allows.

The service is professional for the most part, although the last time I was there, a minor skirmish broke out between the servers. If that continues, they may rename it M's Dine-and-Fight. With its tiny kitchen up front, there's no back-of-the-house where employees can let down their hair in private, which can be disturbing or entertaining depending on the turn of events.

My favorite meal at M's is a good glass of wine, a caesar salad, and the establishment's great Greek sandwich, made of ground turkey, blended with walnuts, herbs, and spices—an exquisite light meal. I also like the paté sandwich, and the Kosher hot dog. The peanut butter chicken soup is also excellent.

M's does a good luncheon business, particularly on Saturdays when the tourists hit the Old Market. During the week, a number of regulars can be found there. Dress varies from casual jeans to ultra-sophisticated, much the same as in any Old Market eatery.

The dinner menu is a bit more complicated, with specials every evening. The chef has a way with soups, and good crusty bread accompanies every meal. You wouldn't come to eat the usual steakhouse fare at M's, but they do claim to have the best tenderloin in town and great rib-eyes served with unique sauces. My preference is for their pasta, veal, poultry, and seafood dishes. Nightly specials can range from blackened redfish with pineapple cream cheese to chicken with a roast red pepper and butter sauce. I've come to expect unusual preparations with great flair.

M's is the perfect place to get revved up for a walk through Old Market shops or mellowed out for an evening at The Orpheum. The creativity of the food and the ambiance will bring you back again and again. M's Pub—impeccable!

Old Vienna Cafe—Omaha

4829 South 24th, 402-733-7491

T o find an authentic South Omaha hangout, go to the Old Vienna Cafe. Hanging on the walls of this old-world-style bistro are photos of local politicos, evidence that anyone aspiring to high office needs to spend time here. In an alcove in the back you can imagine South Omaha pols with big cigars plotting strategy, swapping votes and sipping vintage wines.

The atmosphere is dark with mahogany paneling, Austrian scenes on the walls, and European banners and posters suspended from the ceiling. A collection of wine and beer bottles is crammed into every remaining space. Except for a few tables for bar service near the front door, the dinner tables are set formally with white linen tablecloths, red napkins, and unmatched china. Classical music adds a perfect touch.

The cafe's building has a fascinating history. Twenty years ago the bar on the main floor was a front for a bookie operation on the second floor. The Cafe's current owner and chef, Walter Hecht, showed me a large antique cupboard he brought from upstairs when he started his restaurant ten years ago. In the back of drawers were pockets for stashing cash in the event of a raid. When Walter discovered the envelopes there were a few bills hidden away.

The wine list is extensive, with the traditional European emphasis on age and quality. Walter seems to get a lot of pleasure out of presenting his wine suggestions with each entree, and he has a wide selection to offer. He can offer reasonably-priced house wines by the glass or an extravagant Baron Lafite Rothschild at $385 a bottle.

The food at the Cafe doesn't disappoint. The emphasis is on Austrian and German dishes, particularly veal. Eight different veal dishes are served. The menu has three selections of weinershnitzel and such dishes as Vienna goulash. The entrees are embellished with exquisite sauces.

Whether you're a politician, a bookie, a wine connoisseur, or gourmet you'll enjoy the flavor of South Omaha's version of old Vienna.

Ted and Wally's—Omaha

1115 Howard, 402-341-5827

S how me someone who doesn't enjoy ice cream and I'll show you a grouch. So if you're looking for long faces, don't go into Ted and Wally's ice cream parlor in the Old Market area of Omaha. I guarantee there won't be a grouch in sight. In fact, the first thing you'll notice is that everyone is smiling. That's because ice cream is happiness. To prove it, try this simple test: stick a double dip cone in the hand of a kid of any age and see what happens. See what I mean?

There are lots of things to smile about at Ted and Wally's. The ice cream, labeled "Premium Ice Cream," is rich and creamy. Made right before your eyes in huge churns packed with rock salt and ice, it's a nostalgic trip back to an old-fashioned ice cream shop. But you'll smile not only because Ted and Wally's ice cream tastes good, but also because it gives you a chance to express your creativity. As you wait in line, ponder the blackboard that offers this week's flavors: peppermint stick, cinnamon, even Swiss milk chocolate, and about twenty other selections. If it's August, you might be in a peach mood, or in the spring perhaps some wild whimsy will pull you toward banana bubblegum. Whatever it is, it's your choice and it's fun.

If you're really feeling creative, select a "mix-in"—concoctions made with ice cream and such sweet-tooth delicacies as M&M's, Reese's Pieces, Butterfingers, Snickers, bubblegum, peanuts, almonds, chocolate chips, granola, and coconut. Let your imagination run wild. How about butter pecan ice cream with Snickers mixed in topped with butterscotch chips and coconut? Ahhhhhhh...Fantastic!

In contrast to the mix-ins, which are a new-fangled invention, there are treats for ice cream nostalgia buffs: green rivers, chocolate phosphates, cherry sodas, and egg creams. Plus sundaes galore: maple walnut, dutch chocolate, hot fudge, and spiced apple. Top it off with a strawberry shortcake sundae or a traditional banana split and you'll understand why it's an ice cream lover's paradise.

Ted and Wally's high-ceilinged store, nestled among a cluster of restored historic buildings, is comfortable and spacious, painted a bright white with brick, and fern accents. There are booths and old-fashioned ice cream tables with chairs. The atmosphere is as refreshing as the ice cream.

So if you're walking around Omaha's Old Market and spot people without smiles on their faces, point them toward Ted and Wally's.

Salvatore's—Omaha

4688 Leavenworth, 402-553-1976

Katherine and I hadn't heard much about Salvatore's so we really weren't expecting much. We were expecting even less when we noticed the lava rock on the outside of the building. But dinner at Salvatore's was like reaching into a grab bag and finding a diamond.

Everything about Salvatore's is old-style Italian, even down to the absence of pizza on the menu. Owner, Sam Bonofede, is a talkative and entertaining man who dazzles guests with his tableside banter. Our waiter, a small, dark man with a wonderful mustache, sparkling brown eyes, and boundless energy, was above all a professional who didn't talk much but had developed a bond with us by the end of our meal. The atmosphere is elegant, a little overdone, but reminiscent of an Italian garden. It is quiet, just dark enough, with a touch of romance. The Italian love of wine is also evident; a wine is recommended next to each entree on the menu. And finally there is the enticing aroma of good cooking, the herbs, spices, lemon, and garlic; a smell that is almost good enough to eat.

But if the aromas are heavenly, wait 'til you taste the food. Someone in Salvatore's kitchen really knows what they're doing. Our two antipasto dishes of marinated artichoke hearts and mushrooms and angel hair pasta with a southern Italian tomato sauce were both excellent. But the entree we shared was even better. The veal piccata was thin and tender with a delicate flavor encouraged but not overwhelmed with the traditional sauce of wine, garlic, and lemon. The spiced garlic potatoes on the side were unusual and wonderful.

We raved to each other throughout the meal. During our post-meal evaluation, we agreed that it was the best Italian meal we'd had this side of New York City, in fact, as good as anything we've ever had there and at one third the price. We can't wait to go back and sample some other dishes.

The next time we visit Salvatore's it won't be as much of a surprise, but I'm confident it will be an experience that we will savor and repeat again and again.

V. Mertz—Omaha

1022 Howard, 402-345-8980

In the old days most saloons had only a few wines available by the glass, and they were the standard house swills of red, white, and rose. But then V. Mertz came up with a new idea—the wine bar. In a rather dark, noisy underground location, V. Mertz created an innovative watering hole. Well, the trend has caught on. There are lots of wine bars now, but among the cognoscenti, V. Mertz stands alone.

Dug down in Omaha's Old Market passageway, V. Mertz has found a unique place to ply its trade. A few tables actually spill out into a sidewalk cafe. Tiny bouquets decorate each table, and a profusion of flowers graces the entrance. Atmosphere abounds, but so do crowds. V. Mertz is the place of choice for Omaha's cafe society.

An *Omaha World-Herald* restaurant critic thinks V. Mertz is the best restaurant in Omaha. It's a sophisticated place, not for tourists, he says. In the critic's words, "Jan Bower and her crew are folks who love food, love to share it, have created a unique, petite bistro catering to the knowledgeable, the traveled, those who just know they like creative food preparation in an atmosphere as close to European as any you'll find in this country." If that description fits, give V. Mertz a try.

Claudia's—Omaha
12129 West Center Road
402-330-3320

Owner Jack Churchill, a man who knows continental cuisine, serves Italian and French in this hard-to-find shopping-center location. (My sense of direction has atrophied since Katherine began giving me all of them.) Try unusual specials—ocean scallops on a bed of pureed black beans. Best caesar salad in the Midlands.

Imperial Palace—Omaha
11200 Davenport
402-330-3888

The Omaha restaurant is larger and fancier than its Lincoln counterpart, but both are identical in presenting quality food and outstanding service. You'll enjoy the magnificent decor in this wonderful palace.

Maxine's Red Lion Inn—Omaha
1616 Dodge
402-346-7600

A continental restaurant perched atop the Red Lion Inn. Like E11even in Lincoln, this is the spot for high altitude extravagance. The huge Sunday brunch is popular. A great place for those who crave elevation, and the prices match.

Neon Goose—Omaha
1012 South 10th
402-341-2063

The Neon Goose, like its name, is a paradox: a classy junk shop (above one of the tables is a deer's head with a violin in its antlers) with sophisticated food. The wide-ranging menu is highlighted by "the freshest seafood flown in daily." Also serves duck, but no goose except for "goosebumps" (deep-fried cheese) or the "goose garden" (a chef's salad). I eat so much I have to waddle out.

Ross's—Omaha
909 South 72nd
402-393-2030

Ross's (established 1956) ranks right up there with Dreisbach's and Johnny's as one of Nebraska's top steakhouses. Its owners pay up to $110 a pound for top corn-fed beef and have bought the Ak-Sar-Ben Champion beef for the last ten years. That's a lot to pay for beef, but it shows Ross's determination to serve only **the best**. A Texas-size place (ranchers bet on how much hay it would hold), but with remarkable elegance for its size. Some variety on the menu, but ordering anything but beef here is like ordering pork chops in Maine.

Acknowledgements

Many people have contributed to the writing of this book. Foremost is Bill Kloefkorn whose delight in nurturing others has been inspiring. Next is Charles Stubblefield who helped shape our thoughts over many a meal. Family, old chums and new-found friends provided much-needed advice and technical assistance: Les Remmers, Monica Mercer, Linda Messman, Angie Johnson, Susan Glendenning, Bob Schultz, Tim Mohanna, Jerry Kromberg, Alan Boye, John Peterson, Louis Brauer, Hazel Brauer, Kent Endacott, Dorothy Pritchard Endacott and Annette Windhorn have been generous with their time and talents. Without the enthusiasm and encouragement of countless other supper scouts around the state, this book would never have been finished. And to all the men and women who cook and serve, we are grateful.